A Job-by-

Wendy Straker

Avon, Massachusetts

For my husband, Brett,
who restored my belief in Happily Ever After

Published by
Polka Dot Press, an imprint of
Adams Media, an F+W Publications Company
57 Littlefield Street, Avon, MA 02322
www.adamsmedia.com

ISBN: 1-59337-495-X
Printed in the United States of America.

J I H G F E D C B A

Library of Congress Cataloging-in-Publication Data
Straker, Wendy.
Men at work : a job-by-job search for Mr. Right / by Wendy Straker.
p. cm.
ISBN 1-59337-495-X
1. Mate selection. 2. Men—Psychology. 3. Man-woman relationships.
4. Professions—Psychological aspects. I. Title.
HQ801.S86 2006
646.7'7082—dc22
2005026068

Acknowledgments

A special thanks to all of the women and men who shared their past and present relationships with me; this book would not have been possible without you.

Many thanks to:

My agent, Tara Mark, for believing in this project.

My editors—Danielle Chiotti and Kirsten Amann, for their incredible enthusiasm and support throughout this process.

My California cheering section.

And last but certainly not least, my mom, dad, and brother, Dave, for their constant praise and support.

Contents

Introduction

You're single, successful and on the dating circuit. In the last two months you've nixed two overworked lawyers (actually both guys canceled your date at the last minute), a struggling entrepreneur (his business went under), and a musician (he started making out with another woman onstage). Now you're being set up with a doctor.

"A doctor!" your friend says. "Dating a doctor is horrible. He'll be 'on call' at least twice a week and when he's not on call, he'll be 'postcall,' which is code for 'disinterested in everything you say.' Oh, and don't expect him to have any social skills. Doctors hardly get outside, they're always pale, and they won't make a dime until they're at least thirty-five."

Okay, so maybe she's right. But there is a flip side. Doctors don't take business trips, which means he won't be away that much, and they never entertain clients, which means he won't be expensing lap dances at a strip club. Plus, he'll make a good living, eventually (yes, you can send your hypothetical kids to private school)—and, best of all, he can prescribe medicine! And that's when it hits you. You can tell a lot about the guy you're about to meet by factoring in what he does for a living.

Think about it. Wall Street traders love to wine and dine (that is, show off their money and connections). They pick the best restaurants, they always order bottled (not tap) water, and they love to keep your drinks coming. Lawyers cancel plans at the last minute (note: always have backup plans) and when they do show up, they keep one eye on their BlackBerry at all times, in case they are called back to the office. Agents rub shoulders with movie stars, but will constantly answer their cell phone throughout your meal (don't be surprised if he sits through dinner with his earpiece in his ear), and doctors need thirty minutes to unwind before they can hold a nice, normal conversation (okay, maybe forty-five). And there is so much more!

So what does this mean for you? It means stop reading your potential guy's horoscope to test out your compatibility and start reading *Men at Work*. Finally you can prepare for the guy you're dating. You'll be able to find out his hours (will he have time for you?), his potential salary (can he afford you?), the risk factors (the number of hot women at his office), plus what he really needs from you when he gets home from work. From the silly details like whether he'll be a cell phone abuser, a BlackBerry user, or a pager kind of guy to the downright serious—how often he will have to cancel plans, travel on business, entertain clients at strip clubs, etc. For those of you who are wondering where all the good men are, duh—they're working! So, isn't it about time you understood exactly what that means?

part 1: The Suits

There's something incredibly sexy about a guy who wears a suit to the office. And regardless of what his title is (he could be a lowly assistant for all you know), a guy in a suit appears professional, dedicated, and willing to provide. Sadly, part of the reason he looks so cute is in fact because he's in uniform (which leaves less room for personal style, AKA, a potential fashion faux pas). So, before you go falling in love with your supposed dream guy, make sure you know how he dresses outside of the office. "A guy in a suit can be very deceiving," says Cheryl. "Because unless you've seen him on the weekends, chances are you have no idea how he dresses outside of work. A friend of mine fell for a lawyer she'd been dating, and after going out with him four times, all of which he came to dinner wearing a suit and tie, she decided to join him for the weekend. Unfortunately this was when his true colors came out. Her somewhat conservative dream guy had traded in his dark blue suit for a worn-out Jerry Garcia T-shirt, a button-down beige cardigan, Birkenstock sandals, cutoff acid-wash jeans and a gold hoop earring!"

the lowdown

his job	personality traits	most commonly used gadget	how he spends his weekends	his biggest concern
lawyer	intelligent, focused, anal	BlackBerry	at the office	making partner
investment banker	focused, detailed, anal	BlackBerry	at the office	getting rich
Wall Street trader	assertive, impulsive, exciting	cell phone	living it up	how "the market" is doing
talent agent	charming, persuasive	cell phone	reading scripts, schmoozing people	closing deals
consultant	knowledgeable, versatile, project-oriented	cell phone	relaxing	keeping the client happy
entrepreneur	creative, passionate, excited	cell phone	working at home	succeeding

chapter 1 The Corporate Lawyer

His accomplishments are impressive and he lets you know that almost immediately. He's intelligent, articulate, and confident—qualities that you find extremely sexy. On paper he's your dream guy, but in person he seems so intense! He checks his e-mail and voice mail three times before your appetizers arrive. When he looks up at you, it's to ask you questions: your interests, upbringing, dislikes, goals, etc. A part of you feels like you're being interrogated. When the entrées arrive, he's outside on a work call, and as soon as you finish dinner he's waving down the waitress for the check. At this point you feel nothing for him; he's cold, distant, and intense. But then it happens. He looks deep into your eyes and tells you that he's sorry. He wishes he didn't have to cut the evening short, but he's been called back to the office. And in that split second, you feel something. He seems different, almost vulnerable, and when he kisses you on the cheek and wishes you a good night, you find yourself hoping he'll call you later.

Unfortunately, when he gets into that company car, he's back on his cell phone and completely focused on work. It's not his fault. He's under so much pressure that he's forced to shift back into work mode. You'll likely re-enter his thoughts the minute he leaves the office.

His Look

Suit and tie, if he's coming from a meeting. Otherwise it's slacks and a button-down. Lawyers dress sharp but professional. The last thing he wants is to be noticed for the wrong reasons.

His Vibe

Driven and intense. Lawyers at top law firms work in abusive, high-pressure environments for years before they reach the top. In the early stages of his career, he has no control over his life and is constantly at the mercy of the partners. If he's got his eyes on making partner, though, this lifestyle will not deter him, making him one of the most ambitious, dedicated guys you've ever met.

His Hours

It depends on how many deals he's working on. On good days he'll be in the office at 8 A.M. and out of work by 8 P.M. On bad days (if he's closing a deal) he could easily be at work until 2 A.M. Chances are he won't know when he'll get out of work so if he calls you at the last minute and says that he can meet you for dinner, go see him! He can't plan much further in advance than that. His schedule is completely unpredictable, so don't expect him to commit to anything; unfortunately, this even includes important family functions. Get used to late dinners, canceled trips, and weekends at the office. The good news is that once he makes partner, his weekends are his! Or, at the very least, he can spend them by your side, working from his (AKA, *your*) country house.

Risk Factor

When you do see him, it is likely he's spent the entire day getting kicked around by partners in the firm. On good days, this leaves him weary but still happy to spend his free time with you. On bad days, expect him to appear exhausted and somewhat disheartened. Be sure to give him some extra love and attention when this happens. You'll be amazed how fast his mood will change.

Perks

He makes a good living (starting salary for those just out of law school is upwards of $100,000), and chances are he likes nice things and wants you to have them too. He's also smart, driven, and ambitious, all qualities that make him extremely sexy. Note: Partners at top law firms make millions of dollars.

Where Will Your Partner Make Partner?

Here's a look at the top five most prestigious law firms:

Wachtell, Lipton, Rosen & Katz (New York): Get ready for huge paychecks (yes!) complete with free electronic gadgets and home Internet access (no!), a full-service kitchen staff, and moving expenses. Expect your guy to have long, unpredictable hours, and a gruesome training program. The good news is that this is one of the most prestigious law firms in the world and the company stresses teamwork, respect, and dedication.

Cravath, Swaine & Moore (New York, London): Cravath is known to be an ultraformal, intense, and somewhat pretentious working environment (rumor has it that the partners have huge egos), though associates claim it's not as stuffy as you might think. Expect your guy to receive a signing bonus, subsidized gym membership, and access to the on-site child care center (a huge plus down the line).

Sullivan & Cromwell (locations include New York, Palo Alto, Washington, D.C., Paris, Sydney, and Beijing): A formal though not necessarily stuffy culture. Sullivan & Cromwell's clients are mostly Wall Street banks. Expect your guy to work long hours and if he's just starting out, chances are he'll be sharing his office space. Sullivan lacks office space, leaving most associates with officemates for up to three years. The good news? Sullivan is known to give its associates lots of responsibilities and opportunities to grow. Plus, they have a great training program!

Skadden, Arps, Slate, Meagher & Flom (locations include Boston, Chicago, Houston, San Francisco, Tokyo, Moscow, and Frankfurt):

Thought of as "the Cancun of law firms," Skadden is an extremely social environment but is also known to be a bit volatile (plenty of screaming partners). Still, Skadden has a close-knit family feel, with associates joining one another for drinks at least once a week. Other perks include weekly attorney lunches, in-house gyms, and up to a $3,000 allowance for tech goodies and Internet access.

Davis Polk & Wardwell (locations include Madrid, Hong Kong, New York, and Menlo Park, CA):

Regarded as one of the most respectful and pleasant places to work, Davis Polk prides itself on creating a healthy work/life balance. Though your guy might occasionally have to cancel plans with you at the last minute (like most other lawyers), Davis Polk does its best to keep this to a minimum. Other perks include great training programs and lots of pro bono work, which keeps things interesting.

Will You Rule Him Out?

Before you decide, here's a look at what to expect when you are dating a corporate lawyer.

Rule #1:
He will have to cancel plans with you at the last minute.

Julie, a corporate lawyer in Manhattan says, "I've seen this scenario a hundred times. The guy is stressed and has to cancel plans on his girlfriend. He feels terrible about it but his girlfriend makes him feel worse. Eventually, he feels like he can't handle the relationship and he lets it go. He's under too much pressure and it's not like he can quit his job. I try to explain this to my nonlawyer friends all the time. It's not like he wants to cancel plans with you; he doesn't have a choice. Sadly, lawyers have no control over their schedules and there's not a lot of consistency in the office either. They're constantly working with new people and so it's not like they get used to working with the same personalities. These guys are also moody. It could be a 5 P.M. call that screws up his dinner plans or a huge deal that he gets put on at the last minute. And once he's been called to do something, there's honestly nothing he can do about it. He can't get out of work for any excuse in the world. If there's a funeral he can, or maybe if he's in a wedding. Otherwise, forget it."

Rule #2:
He will expect you to understand when he's running late, but he'll have a hard time understanding when you are.

According to Sara, who dated her boyfriend for three years before he made partner: "If we had plans and I was late, he would go nuts. I think it was because he had such little control at the office and so he needed to have control of his free time. I also know that in his mind, my job wasn't as important as his was, and therefore there was no excuse for me to make him wait around." Yes, he hates having to postpone plans with you but at the same time he also expects you to understand that this is the nature of his job. Unfortunately, he'll have a hard time understanding if you're running late, leaving him waiting for you. Though it's completely unfair, many lawyers become hypersensitive about what they see as "their time," so he may interpret your tardiness as disregard for the pressure he's under or how much he's sacrificing to spend his time with you. Try not to take this too personally. It has nothing to do with you and everything to do with the stress of his job and his desire to succeed. If you can help it, call ahead of time to let him know you're running late.

Rule #3:
He will touch his cell phone as much as he touches you.

Some guys wake up and instinctively turn over to give their girlfriend a kiss on the cheek; other guys reach for their cell phone or BlackBerry. It's a sad, but an unfortunate fact of his line of work. "My boyfriend wouldn't cuddle with me until he had looked at all his new messages from the night before," says Kate, who is no longer with that guy. "He carried it everywhere and he used to check it at family dinners, weddings, you name it." According to Stacy, another ex-girlfriend, "It's the grown-up guy's version of a blankie. I don't think it matters what line of work he's in, the BlackBerry is his number one love. I was on a trip with my ex last year and when we got to the resort in the Caribbean, his BlackBerry didn't work. I thought we were going to have to return home because he was so panicked. He spent the first half of the day on the phone with the office. They had a new BlackBerry sent by FedEx the following morning."

It may seem like your guy's relationship with his personal e-mail device is more important than his relationship with you, but this is a simple fact of his line of work. Try to remember that he doesn't necessarily want it to be this way—if he's worth your time at all, he won't let you forget that.

Rule #4:

He will treat the partners at his law firm better than he treats you.

He acts as if these guys are God. He constantly asks himself, *Am I good enough to make partner? Will this ever happen for me?* Sadly, lawyers are not up for partner for at least nine years (which is a pretty long courting process), and even then very few people make it. It's an extremely competitive environment and lawyers have to be accessible to the partners at all times, even when they're out of the office. Don't be surprised when he goes above and beyond the call of duty. "There are times when the whole charade drives me crazy," says Hilary. "We had to cut our last vacation short when one of the partners at my boyfriend's law firm invited us to a basketball game. We were in Jamaica with his entire family when Josh got an e-mail from a partner asking if he wanted to go to the Knicks game that Monday night. Another associate was also invited, and since they were both on the partner track, Josh felt it was critical that he attend the game. The minute he got the e-mail, he was in a panic. We stayed for the wedding ceremony, but he spent the rest of the night on the phone with the airlines trying to get us back. We left early the next morning (two days earlier than everyone else). You have no idea what we went through to get back in time. We ended up on a seven-seater plane and I spent the entire ride with my head buried in his shirt because I literally thought we were going to die."

Still, your guy can't help it. His future (and possibly yours) lies in the hands of the partners and he must do anything he can to impress them. Expect him to constantly check his e-mail and voice messages in fear that he will be called back to the office. Don't take it personally when he drops everything the minute he gets called. Maybe it's a 5 P.M. call from the client that screws up his night or a document that gets e-mailed to him as he is walking out the door to meet you. Whatever it is, it's not his fault.

Rule #5:
He will need to be alone when he gets home from work.

Remember this rule; it's true for pretty much any working guy. Sadly, men are not like us. They don't look forward to coming home just so they can cuddle with us after a long day at work. Instead, they look forward to silent time, alone, so that they can zone out in front of the TV. "It's the first time we've been by ourselves all day," says Nick, a typical young lawyer. "It has nothing to do with you and everything to do with the day we just had.

Rule #6:
He'll be thinking about work, even when you're in bed together.

Forget about spooning: your man is going to be tossing and turning all night. Guys can't turn off work as well as we can. They bring it home and they obsess over it all night, especially during those first few minutes before they fall asleep, assuming that they can fall asleep. Sara says, "My boyfriend was so stressed that he developed a chronic cough, which kept us both up all night."

Rule #7:
He'll get frustrated and second-guess his decision to become a lawyer.

This is particularly hard to grasp because you'll wonder why he's working so hard if he hates what he does. Still, your job is to be supportive and sympathetic. Lawyers tend to get depressed in their sixth or seventh year at a law firm. They feel beaten down and deflated, they've worked their butt off in hope of making partner, and yet they have no idea if this will happen for them. This uncertainty makes him doubt his own abilities. He'll grow tired of trying to prove himself and he'll wonder if it will ever be worth it. When he explains to you how meaningless his job is, you'll want to agree (after all, his days are spent shuffling papers and making changes on documents), but try to just listen. Eventually he'll either leave the law firm or he'll get the validation he is searching for.

He Says . . .

We hate having to cancel on you.

"Trust me, we hate disappointing you. We feel terrible and guilty, but the less understanding you are, the more upset we get. We start to panic that we can't handle the extra stress of a relationship and that's when it all falls apart. My last girlfriend would complain to me all the time. She would call me at the office and she'd say things like, 'you better not cancel tonight,' and even though she wouldn't say it meanly, there was this underlying pressure. Every time I had to work late I had a pit in my stomach knowing that she would be upset. Eventually I couldn't take it anymore. She constantly made me feel like I was disappointing her."—Jeff

Go easy on us. We just got our asses kicked at work.

"Some women don't understand what we mean when we say we had a shitty day. We are at the beck and call of the client and the partners. Picture getting scolded because you missed a comma on a thirty-page contract and then having to pretend that you don't mind having to give up courtside Knicks tickets (or whatever it is that makes you as happy as Knicks tickets make me) to spend your night putting "sign here" tabs on twenty boxes of contracts (until 2 A.M.). Then imagine coming into the office the next day, only to find that after thinking about it (for like a minute), the partner decides he doesn't really need to send out those contracts. That's a day in the life of an associate!"—Charles

If we like you, we'll make time to see you.

"Yes, it's hard to find time to date but if we like you, we'll figure something out. Lawyers definitely use work as an excuse to blow off women. It's an easy out without having to hurt your feelings. If we cancel at the last minute, it's probably legit, but if we tell you that we'll 'call you when this deal ends,' that's a sure sign you're being blown off."—Matthew

It doesn't matter how special the plans were. If we have to cancel, we have to cancel, end of story.

"It doesn't matter if the dinner we have to cancel happens to be on the night of our anniversary. We can't go up to a partner and explain that we've been planning this night for two months and it means a lot to our girlfriend. It just doesn't work that way. I think the biggest problem is that women can't possibly understand the pressure of a big law firm unless they work in one. One of my friends married a lawyer and he said it's great because she understands his workload. To everyone else it seems weird that the only way I can get out of work is if someone dies."—Edward

She Says . . .

Do help him out with his work, whenever you can.

"There were times he would come to see me, but he'd have to bring his work with him. During busy times,

I'd help him—he would mark up a document, and I would enter his changes into the computer. It always made me feel good to be a part of his work, even if it was some stupid menial task. Plus, I know that he really appreciated it."—Kate

Do encourage him to meet you for a late dinner, even if you've already eaten.

"He will start to forget that there's an outside world filled with people who are going to dinners, taking trips, and celebrating the holidays. He will be reluctant to book anything because he won't want to disappoint you if he has to cancel. Make sure he gets out every once in a while, even if you have to meet him late for dinner one night a week. I used to meet my boyfriend out at a restaurant and even if I'd already eaten, I'd just sit there and keep him company."—Molly

Don't rely on him for plans.

"You know he's busy, so the best thing to do is to get busy too. You have to be independent and thick-skinned if you want this relationship to work. He will respect that you're not just waiting around to see when his schedule lets up. Make your own dinner plans; even plan your own trips if you have to. Who knows, maybe he'll be able to join you at the last minute."—Jaime

Do understand that his work will always come before you.

"If you're dating a corporate lawyer, he'll always choose his work over you. Make peace with it, or come to terms with the reality that this guy might not be right for you. I come from a home where family always comes first, but my boyfriend always put his job and colleagues ahead of me and his family. That was a difficult adjustment for me, one that ultimately was something I couldn't accept."—Jessica

Don't bank on things changing drastically once he makes partner.

"Sure, he might feel more confident, and more entitled, and he'll certainly feel less panicky and stressed, but he won't feel any less pressure to perform. Instead, he'll want to prove to his fellow partners that he is worthy of his position at the firm."—Alana

The Breakdown

Here's the lowdown on the corporate lawyer:

biggest turn on	He's passionate, intelligent, ambitious, and articulate
biggest challenge	Taking him away from his BlackBerry and getting him to relax
best way to get in touch	BlackBerry–at least you know he checks it
greatest perk	Your mother will be happy
best timing	Once he's made partner

Talking Shop

Here's a list of key words and phrases that will help you speak his language:

The bar exam: No, this has nothing to do with drinking. This is a test your guy must pass before he is able to practice law in a particular state. Note: He gets three tries to pass the bar (JFK Jr. failed the first two times, so don't nix your guy if he doesn't get it right the first time). If he's studying for the bar when you meet him, chances are you won't see him very often.

Billable hour: It's not just hookers and therapists that bill by the hour; lawyers do too. In fact, lawyers could charge as much as $500 an hour, even if he spends that hour talking to his client on the phone. Note: Lawyers have to bill a certain number of hours in order to make partner.

Esquire: This is a title sometimes added to the end of a lawyer's name. If your guy adds the term esquire to his name, beware. Chances are he's a stuffy, pompous individual.

Hung jury: Get your mind out of the gutter!A hung jury is a jury that cannot agree on a verdict by the necessary voting margin.

Interrogation: A form of intense questioning. Lawyers love to interrogate their girlfriends, and half the time they don't even realize they are doing it.

Joint venture: A business relationship undertaken by two or more people engaged in a single defined project. He may refer to your relationship as a "joint venture."

LSAT: The law school entrance exam. It's much like the SATs, but for law school.

Liquid assets: This has nothing to do with his precious wine collection or that vineyard he wants to buy down in Napa. A liquid asset is just an asset that can be quickly or readily converted into cash.

Living trust: No, we're not referring to his (or your) trust issues. A living trust is simply a means of assuring that a decedent's property and assets (for example, his parent's house, savings, etc.) are transferred to his or her heirs according to the decedent's wishes. It's a good sign if your guy has a living trust.

Restraining order: Make sure he doesn't have one of these on his record! A restraining order is an order made by a court to protect an adult (AKA: you) from physical pain or injury, or from being threatened with pain or injury.

Statute of limitations: A legal deadline by which a plaintiff must start a lawsuit. Note: If you have an issue with your boyfriend, bring it to his attention before it's too late. If you wait too long, he might try to tell you that there is a "statute of limitations" on the "crime" he committed and therefore it's no longer up for discussion.

Summer associate: The title law students are given when they intern at a law firm. This is the only time your guy is going to be wined and dined by the firm. Expect him to spend his days lunching at five-star restaurants followed by tickets to sporting events and Broadway plays.

chapter 2

The Investment Banker

He's that handsome guy reading the *Wall Street Journal* across from you on the train. Sadly, he never looks up at you because he's too focused on the page he's reading to even think about the world around him. You watch him closely (it's not freaky or anything because he has no idea you're looking), and you can't help but imagine how much your mother would love him. He's practically made for the top of your wedding cake; he's neat, well dressed, handsome, and professional. When the train slows down he folds up his paper and checks his Ironman watch, and just as he stands up to make it to the exit, you realize that you've actually met him before. In fact, he asked you for your number once, and then waited six months to call, only to schedule a date and then have his secretary cancel five minutes before you were walking out the door. As he exits the train he smiles in your direction but it's obvious he has no idea who you are. Before you get all bummed out, there's something you should know: Your "dream guy" lives at the office, literally. Once he exits that train he goes straight to work and he stays there until 2, sometimes 3 A.M.

His Look

Designer suit, Hermes tie, and a digital Ironman watch. This guy makes a boatload of money and even though he can buy a Rolex without batting an eye, he chooses to wear a $15 digital watch. Why? Because that's what so many other investment bankers do to convince themselves that they're actually down to earth. As for the rest of his attire, it's head-to-toe designer threads. Higher-ups are well put together with perfectly pressed suits. The more junior guys (analysts and even associates) can be found wearing rumpled slacks and wrinkled button-downs, an unfortunate by-product of all-nighters in the office.

His Vibe

Highly intelligent, motivated, and extremely confident. These guys are purely financially driven. They have big egos and they know that someday they'll make a ton of cash. Sadly, they never see the light of day, but then again they chose this path to get rich. Though these guys are incredibly meticulous and anal, they tend to spend a lot of unproductive time in the office (proving their dedication, of course). Late mornings are spent waiting around and shooting the shit, followed by hours in front of the computer screen reviewing Excel spreadsheets, crunching numbers, and stressing over pitch books and models. Except for vice presidents, all investment bankers sit in open cubicles, so even guys in their thirties have little privacy. And that means no personal phone calls! Much like law associates, analysts in investment banks work in high-pressure, verbally abusive environments (some claim that investment banks are more ruthless than law firms), and they are at the beck and call of their clients and superiors. They bow down to the higher-ups and have no control over their schedule.

His Hours

Bankers get in on the later side, around 10 or 11 A.M., and work long nights, sometimes until 3 A.M. or later. Morning hours are always slow (note: this is the only good time to call him) and get progressively busier after lunch, which is typically a forty-five minute trip to the local restaurant (yes, you can meet him for lunch during the day!). By 6 P.M., things are operating at high speed with last-minute changes and updates that could entail being at the office until 3 A.M. Investment bankers practically live in the office, which is why places like Goldman Sachs have huge workout areas, showers, and company cots to sleep on. Analysts get less than four hours of sleep each night, and most of them, regardless of their level, have no social life and few outside interests. Add to that the fact that they spend their entire day staring at their computers and crunching numbers and it's no wonder their personality can seem to get lost in the shuffle.

Risk Factor

He spends his life in the office and when he's not at work he's catching up on sleep. This guy lives and breathes his career and that includes weekends. Expect him to have to cancel plans, reschedule trips, and miss family weddings and other important events. Investment bankers work for the promise of getting rich. They live for the future and not for the moment. And because they spend so much time with their coworkers, office hookups are not that uncommon. It's not unheard of for a married investment banker to leave his wife for an associate or a secretary at the office.

Perks

Flying in the company jet, getting first-class upgrades, accruing frequent flyer miles for that trip to Hawaii, unlimited use of the company car, and great business trips—oh, and did we mention that he makes tons of money? On average, investment bankers make a $500,000 salary within the first five years. And considering that bankers rarely get outside and have had limited opportunities to spend their money, it makes for a nice financial cushion (or, ahem, cushion cut diamond). Note: It takes a lot for an investment banker to get fired those first few years. The hardest part is getting his foot in the door.

The Breakdown

Here's a look at the investment banker:

biggest turn on	He's rich
biggest challenge	Being able to see him, ever
best way to get in touch	Call him at the office before lunch
greatest perk	He can afford nice things
best timing	When he's getting his MBA

The Secretary

He's in a meeting.
Can I put you through to voice mail?

She sees him more times in one day than you do in one week. She knows his habits, his preferences, and the number of women who call him at the office. If he's cheating on you, she knows it. In fact, she could be the one he's cheating with. She's his gatekeeper, and regardless of how undesirable her job may seem, to you she has the most coveted position. So who is this woman? She's his secretary, and according to a number of past girlfriends, you should befriend her.

Secretaries can be found at most law and investment banking firms, and they're typically easy to befriend. Jessica, a corporate lawyer, says, "Secretaries are usually open to making friends because their bosses (one of which is your boyfriend) are probably real jerks at work and besides that, they're probably pretty bored." So, what should you do? "Learn her name, always ask how she's doing, comment on the weather, ask about her kids and grandkids, playfully make fun of your boyfriend with her (they love that!), pretend to confide in her. Once you've established a relationship with her, she will begin to reveal important details. You'll find out who he's traveling with on business, if he's really in a meeting when he says he is, and what kind of mood he'll be in when he comes home."

Will You Rule Him Out?

Before you decide, here's a look at what to expect when you are dating an investment banker.

Rule #1:

He will have no control over his life.

He works insane hours, including weekends. He might be walking out of the office on his way to catch a plane for your one-year anniversary trip when a partner stops him at the elevator to tell him he's been put on a new deal, and he will be expected to cancel his plans. Investment bankers must always be accessible. They all have a company BlackBerry and they're always on call. Don't expect him to take you to the movies, ever. Two hours plus previews is an eternity for this guy. Much like corporate lawyers, investment bankers are at the mercy of their clients. If you're really serious about him, ask your guy what he wants out of life. For some of these guys, their lives are all about work. Others plan on leaving this environment later down the line, once they strike it rich. Ask him if he wants this life forever, or if it's a temporary thing. If he plans on staying in this career, you need to plan on not seeing him the majority of the time.

Rule #2:

He will appear asexual for extended periods of time.

This is a sad fact, but one that's worth noting. Many investment bankers leave the office feeling drained. Unlike their creative counterparts (i.e., agents, actors, musicians, entrepreneurs), their work is not exciting. What does this mean for you? It means he's not getting any sort of adrenaline rush at the office so there's simply nothing to get his energy up. "When he had a big deal or a big day ahead, there would be no kissing or sex," says Laurie. "He was way too stressed." According to a number of ex-girlfriends, sex with their investment banker boyfriends was far from spontaneous. "One time I went to his office at 8 P.M. and no one was around," says Michelle. "He looked so cute sitting there in his suit, staring so intently at his computer, so I went over to his desk chair and tried to straddle him. He completely freaked out! He was way too wound up and focused on work to let go sexually."

Rule #3:
Most bankers are particular about their likes and dislikes.

Remember, his job is incredibly detail-oriented, which means that he has to be highly organized and methodical. What does this mean for you? Chances are he has a system and an opinion for everything and that includes decisions around the house. Don't be surprised if he insists on joining you at Bloomingdales to pick out your china pattern!

Rule #4:
He won't want to sleep at your apartment, ever.

Guys in general hate sleeping at their girlfriend's apartment and investment bankers are no exception. They work late nights, sometimes until 3 A.M., and the last thing they'll want to do is head over to your apartment only to worry about getting up early so that they can go back to their place and shower before work. And these guys are particular, remember? They like their own stuff (i.e., soaps, towels, sheets). Cara says, "I have a perfectly good apartment, but I swear there's no need for it. I think in the last six months, my boyfriend has literally slept in my bed once . . . and that was when he took a nap! I've probably slept in my bed four times. And to top it off, my apartment is much closer to his office than his is."

Rule #5:

The more successful he becomes the more obsessive and anal he will be.

Higher-ups are meticulous and finicky. Don't be surprised if his button-down shirts are color-coded according to shades of blue. These guys are incredibly structured. They rarely hit the snooze button (and if they do, they've planned to do so by setting the alarm nine minutes earlier than when they have to get up), they're very concerned with being in good shape (he probably works out every day), and they're obsessed with personal hygiene. Chances are he has a morning cleansing ritual filled with high-end skin products and scented shampoos. Did somebody say *American Psycho?* "I dated an MD (managing director) a few times and when I went over to his apartment I found his bathroom filled with scented soaps, exfoliants, masks, and shaving creams complete with shaving brushes," says Julie. "And that was just the beginning. His closets were custom-made, his shoeboxes had Polaroid pictures of his shoes on the front of them, and his button-downs were color coordinated! Worse, when I walked in for the first time, he made me take off my shoes and leave them in the hallway. They were my Jimmy Choos!"

Rule #6:

He'll make ridiculously insane amounts of money.

Ah, yes, the plus side of dating an investment banker. This guy makes so much money that technically he could retire by the time he's forty. The average investment banker makes half a million dollars by his fifth year. Add bonuses to that, plus the fact that he never has time to spend his own money, and you're looking at a pretty cushy existence. But just because he's rich doesn't mean he's generous. There are plenty of cheap investment bankers out there. And there's nothing worse than a frugal rich guy.

Rule #7:

He will constantly postpone plans.

Maybe it's a new deal that throws off his plans, or last-minute changes to a pitch book for tomorrow's meeting. Whatever the case may be, when things get hectic, this guy goes into a different zone, one that doesn't include you. Ask him to let you know as soon as he suspects he'll be swamped. It's better for him to be up-front about it right away than to string you along until the last minute. "My ex-boyfriend would make plans to meet with me at a specific time, then twenty minutes before we were supposed to meet he'd call from the office and postpone. I'd be sitting on my couch all dressed up, watching reruns of *That '70s Show*, and he'd keep pushing the time back until I'd get so tired of waiting that I'd end up falling asleep. And when I'd call the next morning, he'd say, 'Don't get mad at me. I haven't even left the office.'"

He Says . . .

What's so bad about dating a guy who works hard?

"Just because we're focused on our careers it doesn't mean we're not focused on you. In fact, most guys I know work harder when they find the woman they want to marry because they want to be able to provide for her. It's not like we're out there cheating. Instead, we are traveling to some random city with a bunch of clients, trying to make deals happen. There are bad guys out there and then there are guys who want to provide for their families. Being with a guy who works hard is not such a bad thing."—Aaron

If a client wants to go to a strip club, I'm going to take him to one.

"Put yourself in our shoes. If I am with a client and we are working on a major deal and he wants me to take him to a strip club, of course I am going to take him to a strip club. It doesn't mean that I want to do it, but if I am doing business with this guy and he wants something, I am going to make sure he gets it. Honestly, I wish every woman would get a lap dance so that she could realize how impersonal it really is. The woman barely looks at you, she does some cheesy moves with her boobs in your face, and then she moves on to the next guy. Seriously, there is nothing sexy about it."—Jason

Don't expect us to be mushy on the phone with you.

"We can't be all mushy with you when we're at work. If you call and we're abrupt, don't take it personally. It's because we're busy, not because we care about you less than we did yesterday. If we say 'I'm in a meeting,' it means that we're in a meeting."—Jared

She Says . . .

His work is his life.

"You have to love him so much that the work stuff doesn't matter. If you are willing to be with the man you love only when he is free to give himself to you, then it's worth it. Get used to late-night dinners and going to events by yourself. Just try not to take it too personally."—Julie

Find out what his priorities are.

"Some of these guys want to work in investment banking when they're single, but once they have a family, they want to move on and find a nicer, more realistic work schedule. Find out what your guy wants out of life. If he wants to stay in investment banking, chances are you won't see him very much. Make sure you are okay with this."—Molly

Talking Shop

Here's a list of key words and phrases that will help you speak his language:

Acquisition: The process of taking over or "acquiring" a controlling interest in another company. Acquisition also describes any deal where the bidder ends up with 50 percent or more of the company taken over. If your investment banker boyfriend is working on an acquisition deal, chances are he's going to be working late at the office.

Analyst training program: AKA your own personal hell. The analyst training program is a gruesome two-year program for analysts who enter investment banking straight out of college. This is probably the worst time to date an investment banker. Expect him to pull plenty of all-nighters, which means nights away from you. Seriously, these guys are known to sleep under their desks. Note: Most analysts return to school for their MBA once they have finished the training program.

BIMBO: No, it's not what you think. BIMBO stands for "Buy-in management buyout." A BIMBO enables a company to reshuffle its capital to bring about a change in management. Essentially, a group of managers will acquire enough share capital to "buy out" the company from within. Still don't understand? Just know it has nothing to do with another woman!

Buyout: The purchase of a company or a controlling interest of a corporation's shares. This often happens when a company's existing managers wish to take control of the company. Again, this could be a crazy time at the office. Expect long hours and late nights if his company is working on a buyout.

Due diligence: A phrase used to describe all the research your guy will do on a company before deciding whether or not to invest in it. He will constantly be performing "due diligence," which includes everything from meeting with accountants to go over a company's books, looking at past decisions the company has made, and making projections of its future success. Due diligence could take months, even years.

Exit strategy: A way out. No, not out of your relationship! Out of an investment, silly. Investment bankers are always looking for an exit strategy so that they don't get stuck investing in something for too long. If a fund manager can't see an obvious way out of a potential investment, then he won't invest in it.

Live deal: Live deals are deals that are in the middle of negotiations. Your guy could have three or four live deals going on at one time. This is the most stressful time for an investment banker. Expect him to work late nights and weekends during a live deal.

Turnaround: This is not a term you want to hear unless, of course, you are in bed together. When this term is used in reference to investment banking, it relates to a certain finance that is provided to a company with severe financial difficulties. The aim is to provide enough capital to bring a company back from the brink of collapse.

chapter 3

The Wall Street Trader

He works with money, which usually means that he'll make a ton of it. Yippee! He also knows all the late-night hot spots, and for your date, he'll probably reserve the best table at one of the most popular restaurants followed by box seats to a Broadway show or major sporting event. This guy has incredible connections and he's encouraged to use them, so expect to be seriously wined and dined.

Traders love the good life, and when they're not in the office, they can be found "solidifying their business relationships," which involves entertaining clients or being entertained by clients. Either way, these guys are social and charismatic. And they're used to getting anything they want, the minute they want it. These guys have so much money, so many connections, and loads of free time, it's no wonder that they're always looking for the next best thing. And yes, in some cases, that includes women as well. Traders have a short attention span and the minute they grow bored with one gadget (whether that be a flat-screen TV or a three-month relationship with you), they're on to the next. So, proceed with caution.

His Look

These guys like the finer things in life. They know what money buys and they want to have those things. Though Wall Street is less showy and formal than it used to be, these guys still care about their threads. Bigwigs in old-school firms can still be found in custom-made suits complete with designer shoes and a shirt to match, and traders who work on the sell side of the business usually wear suits and ties when they're outside of the office. Though most traders dress well, there's still a cheesy salesmanlike quality to this business, so don't be surprised if you meet a trader who seems more like a used-car salesman and less like Mr. Big. Note: The newbies in this business are the young ones that try too hard. They can be found wearing Gucci sunglasses, driving a Mercedes convertible (even when it's fifty degrees outside), sporting a gold Rolex, and talking about their summer cottage in the Hamptons. The successful, confident ones seem to care the least about showing off.

His Vibe

Confident, cocky, wealthy, and smooth. Wall Street is still a boys' club, so when there's an attractive woman in the office, the flirtatious comments are out of control. Though these guys might act like gentlemen with you at first—they'll take your coat, pull out your chair, and order your dinner—don't think they won't try to get down your pants later. Traders have huge egos and they are so used to getting what they want that after a while they start to believe they can buy anything, even you. As for life on the trading floor, it's insanely busy. If things get crazy while he's on the phone with you, most likely he'll hang up, or he might put you on hold while he plays with other people's money—which is a major turn on (who needs phone sex when you can listen to him buy and sell stocks?). When he's not busy, expect him to instant message you five times in a row. This guy thrives in a fast-paced, highly energetic environment. If there's a moment of silence he will need to fill it to keep his adrenaline going, even if that means stalking you over instant message. Sadly, the minute you respond he's busy trading again.

His Hours

Sell-side traders get in as early as 6 A.M., whereas buy-side traders get started between 7 A.M. and 8 A.M. Though these guys get to work ridiculously early, they also get out earlier. Expect him to be out of the office by 5 P.M. at the latest, which leaves him just enough time to go to the gym and take a nap before he heads out for a client dinner. Whatever you do, never call a trader during opening bell (9:30 to 10 A.M.) or closing bell (4 to 4:30 P.M.). Note: Traders never take a lunch break (sometimes they don't even have time to go to the bathroom); instead, they order in and eat at their desks.

Risk Factor

These guys don't need to work hard to get what they want. Add to that the fact that they're impatient, and it's no wonder they have a reputation for being players. Though this guy might seem spontaneous and romantic, when he calls you at a moment's notice with front row tickets to a Broadway show or box seats to a sporting event, the reality is that these tickets were placed on his desk fifteen minutes before he called. So, what may seem like the greatest date in the world may actually have nothing to do with the guy you are dating (or how much he likes you) and everything to do with his profession. Chances are he's taking out a different woman every night. Why? Because he can. Note: Traders never travel for work (the research sales side might, but not the traders themselves), and they never need to go into the office over the weekend. If a trader tells you that he has to work over the weekend or take a business trip, chances are he's lying.

Perks

He knows how to live the good life and his work allows him to do just that. This guy works great hours, with phenomenal perks—yes, you will be able to take part in this. Plus he never has to work weekends or travel for business. And, if all goes well in the market, chances are he'll make a phenomenal living. Find a faithful trader and you've hit the jackpot!

The "Client" Dinner

"We'd often get into fights after he took me to a client dinner. He felt that I wasn't impressive enough. He always made me feel as if I had to perform."—Stacy

Whether he's asking you to have dinner at his boss's house or to join him at a Lakers game with a client and his wife, the work function date is one of the most important tests in the beginning of any relationship. Think you're a natural when it comes to social situations? Think again. This guy has a long list of don'ts that you might not even realize.

- **Don't share your religious or political views**—The last thing he wants is for you to offend his client. Though it may sound trivial, people get intense when they discuss politics or religion, so it's best not to get into a heated debate, even if you think it's innocuous. Tracy had been on five dates with Jon before he invited her to his client's house for dinner: "His client asked my opinion about something in politics that I happened to be very familiar with. I thought we were having an intelligent conversation, but apparently Jon didn't agree. He later told me that he'd been kicking me under the table to get me to stop talking."
- **Don't outshine the client or his wife**—Though he may have trouble telling you this, he doesn't want you to monopolize the conversation or attract too

much attention. That means no thigh-high boots, short skirts, or low-cut sweaters. "If anything, you should wear less makeup and pull your hair back," says Jeff, a Wall Street trader. "We might be entertaining some pretty powerful people and we want them to feel comfortable. The best thing you can do is to bond with our client's wife or girlfriend. Make her feel comfortable, ask her questions, and let her steer the topic of conversation."

- **Don't appear bored**—Client dinners are not always about courtside seats or fabulous five-star restaurants. And the people your boyfriend entertains might not be that hip or fun either. Whatever you do, don't pout. "There's nothing worse than having to worry about whether your girlfriend is miserable," says Jason, a sales trader. "We know that these things can be a drag sometimes, but we desperately need you to make us look better, not worse."
- **Don't have too much to drink**—You need to appear poised and in control, and we all know how difficult that is when we've had one too many. Remember, these people are not your friends and no matter how comfortable you feel, you are still there for business purposes. If he catches you slurring your words or revealing something a little too personal, he's going to be mortified.

Will You Rule Him Out?

Before you decide, here's a look at what to expect when you are dating a Wall Street trader.

Rule #1:

He's used to making massive decisions in a matter of seconds.

These guys are used to processing insane amounts of information in a short period of time. They operate at a very fast pace and they like to get things done quickly. Their phone conversations never entail the common pleasantries that most people begin with before getting to the heart of a conversation. Instead, his mentality is "give me the information—*let's go.*" There's no thinking about things or mulling things over. He'll never have meetings to discuss a plan of action; instead, he will make his decision in a matter of seconds, and most of the time that decision will involve hundreds of thousands of dollars. What does this mean for you? He's impulsive and incredibly self-assured, even when he's wrong. He's also used to getting what he wants when he wants it. Don't be surprised if he goes out to buy milk and comes home with a new $100,000 car.

Rule #2:

He shares his phone line with a bunch of traders.

Most traders don't have their own phone lines at work and regardless, they have no privacy. They are literally within earshot of a bunch of people they know, which means that everyone can hear your phone conversation. "I try not to call him at work because I never know which guy is going to answer the phone," says Kara. "Plus, you never know the pace of the office. Sometimes things are really calm and then in a matter of seconds with no warning whatsoever, it will get crazy and he'll have to practically hang up on me. Understand that this is his work environment and it has nothing to do with you. If I really need him, I'll send him an instant message and just say something like, 'you there?' and if he's busy he'll write back a one-liner like 'jammed' or 'slammed' and I'll know that he'll get in touch with me when things ease up."

Rule #3:

You need to be a team player. His job is all about building relationships.

He will have client dinners and functions almost every night and occasionally on the weekends. When he brings you along, he'll expect you to act a certain way. "You have to remember that no matter how comfortable you might feel with his clients, these are business colleagues and they are not friends," says Hilary. "My boyfriend used to prep me before a client dinner. He'd tell me what to expect and what his client's wife was like, what she was interested in, etc. It's all about making those people feel comfortable and letting them steer the conversation." Though many of these events will involve you, others will not. Rachel says, "My fiancé used to play golf every Saturday morning at 7:30 A.M. with one of his clients. I wasn't thrilled about it because it was the weekend and I wanted to spend time with him, but I didn't have much choice. For a while I pouted about it and I slept in while he took off for the mornings. Then I realized that unless I started taking up golf, I wasn't going to be able to see him. So, that's what I did. I took golf lessons in the morning and then when he was finished playing with his client, we would meet up and have lunch together. I ended up really liking it too. You have to make a lot of compromises when it comes to relationships, regardless of what career your guy is in."

Rule #4:

He won't want to sleep at your apartment, ever.

Not only do these guys have to get up very early (as early as 5:30 A.M.), but many of them need to have access to their home computers in case they have to trade overseas. "My computer is my baby," says Joe. "There are times when I need to trade from my apartment, and even if the woman I'm dating has a computer, it's not going to have the capabilities and software programs that I need. Women have trouble understanding that. But nonetheless, I just can't do it. It's too much of an inconvenience to sleep out."

Rule #5:

Just because he takes you on the best dates, doesn't mean he's really into you.

These guys will take you on better dates than any other guy in any other industry. They will wine and dine you from the moment you step into their company car to the minute you step out. Expect him to take you to the U.S. Open finals, the U2 concert, the Super Bowl . . . you name it. Though traders may seem spontaneous and romantic, the truth is that they've been offered these tickets moments before they called you, and their biggest challenge was being able to fill them. So before you get all weak in the knees, remember, though he might be that into you, these perks have nothing to do with it.

Rule #6:
He will be multitasking while he's on the phone with you.

These guys have a million things going on at one time and they're great at juggling a number of tasks at once (in some cases, that skill translates into being able to date a number of women). Still, things do get crazy at the office, so don't be surprised if he's sending instant messages, taking phone calls, or simply cutting you off midsentence by screaming a series of numbers followed by commands to buy or sell. It's actually pretty sexy. When things get really crazy, chances are he'll scream "gotta run!" into the phone and just hang up. Don't take this personally. It has nothing to do with you.

Rule #7:
Most traders have very little patience.

Traders work in extremely fast-paced environments where millions of dollars change hands in a matter of seconds. They are not overthinkers simply because they can't be (they don't have the time). Instead traders are taught to trust their gut and react almost instantly. As a result, these guys can be seen as somewhat impulsive outside of the office. Don't expect him to spend hours mulling over a decision, and at the same time, don't expect him to wait patiently while others take their time to make things happen. This is not his fault and yet it can still be incredibly frustrating for you. After all, he's pretty used to having thing go exactly as he expects them to. Think about it. Traders don't have to work long hours, they know when the market opens and closes, they never have to revise memos, prepare presentations, travel, work weekends, etc. If you can, calmly remind him that the outside world doesn't operate at the pace of Wall Street.

He Says . . .

The last thing we want to do when we get home from work is talk on the phone.

"Remember, we've just spent our entire day hitting the phones and making calls. The last thing we want to do when we come home is get on the phone with you. Don't take this personally. It has nothing to do with you. We need to zone out, go to the gym, relax. Our days are so fast-paced. We need to decompress before we head back out to a client dinner."—Chris

Wall Street isn't as wild as it used to be.

"Yes, we used to have a pretty bad reputation and lots of times it was true. There was excessive partying, strip clubs, private planes, you name it. But it's not as excessive anymore.

First, because there are so many more women on Wall Street than there used to be. And second, because a New York law was just passed against 'excessive entertainment,' which means we can no longer expense a $2,000 night at a strip club. Maybe $500, but not $2,000. They've tightened up on the whole Wall Street culture. No more lewd comments to the secretary and no more shagging her at the company party! Plus, everything is monitored now. So that means no dirty e-mails, instant messages, or surfing porn!"—Rob

The market is not going to slow down for you.

"Women don't understand that when a trader answers the phone and tells you he's busy, it means he is busy. End of story. We work in such a dynamic, fast-paced environment where in a split second millions of dollars are either made or lost. And unfortunately, the market doesn't slow down for you. It's open when it's open."—Charles

She Says . . .

Don't expect him to send you well-thought-out e-mails.

"Remember, these guys work in such a fast environment that it's unlikely he'll take the time to craft out a love letter to you over e-mail. In fact if he does, you should worry. The truth is that he needs to be focused on the market, not your e-mail. Expect quick, blunt-sounding e-mails filled with spelling errors and incomplete sentences. This has little to do with his level of intelligence and everything to do with the fact that he's multitasking."—Tara

Traders live the good life because they can.

"Traders have the time and the money to do everything completely over the top. Every trader I've ever dated has been a party boy. These are some of the crassest guys I've ever met, but they're also a riot. And they are phenomenal in bed. The only problem is that they're not even close to settling down. Hands down I've had my wildest times with trader boyfriends, but in the end I just wish I could get them to stay at home every once in a while and watch a movie with me."—Julie

At least you know where he is every day!

"Dating a trader beats dating an investment banker or real estate developer. At least you know where this guy is every day, and you know that he gets out of work shortly after the market closes. These guys never have to travel for work, and there's no ambiguity. There's none of that 'I am in a meeting' stuff, or 'I am going to be home late because I am at work,' and he'll never work weekends. These guys have teacher hours and they make ten times what teachers make! How can you top that?"—Stephanie

The Breakdown

Here's the skinny on the Wall Street Trader:

biggest turn on	He works with money all day
biggest challenge	Getting him to commit to you
best way to get in touch	Instant message
greatest perk	He knows how to wine and dine
best timing	When the stock market is good

Talking Shop

Here's a list of key words and phrases that will help you speak his language:

Are you open?: No, he's not asking if you are available. Instead 'are you open' is a phrase traders use with other traders, on the phone or over instant message, to find out if a new customer can still participate in a trade.

BRB: Stands for "be right back." Traders rarely send out long e-mails or instant messages. Instead they speak in abbreviations, which may seem abrupt to you but are not meant to be that way. If he can't respond to your IM right away, chances are he'll type "BRB" on your screen.

Back up the truck: No, he's not talking about your booty! This is yet another trader term which means that the seller should prepare for a very large buyer.

Bull market: This has nothing to do with an actual bull nor is it a reference to something being bullshit. A bull market is a financial market in which prices are rising or are expected to rise. All you need to know is that this is a good thing.

Day trader: A stock trader who holds stock positions for a very short time (from minutes to hours) and makes numerous trades each day. Most day traders make trades that are entered and closed out within the same day. Though this was prevalent at the height of the market, now it can be pretty risky. Note: Be careful with this guy. His job is incredibly unstable.

Hammering the market: Before you get too excited, this has nothing to do with your boyfriend's ability to use a hammer. Hammering the market is actually a phrase used to describe the heavy selling of stocks by speculators who think the stock is about to drop.

Opening bell: A bell that rings to signify the beginning of a trading session. Trading sessions begin at 9:30 A.M. every morning, so don't expect to hear from your guy at this time and whatever you do, don't try to get in touch with him during this time either. Note: Closing bell, a bell that rings when the market closes, occurs at 4:30 P.M. and is also not a great time to call your trader boyfriend.

The street: "Here's how it works on the street . . . " Some traders refer to Wall Street as "the street." Though it may seem annoying, it's kind of like New Yorkers calling New York City "the city."

Trading analysts: Babies in the world of Wall Street. Trading analysts are college graduates that have passed the Series 7 exam (an industry licensing exam) and made it through the training program. Starting salary for trading analysts is typically between $45,000 and $55,000 with a year-end bonus of $20,000 to $30,000.

chapter 4

The Talent Agent

You'll either love this guy or you'll hate him, or even worse, you'll have a love-hate relationship with him that leaves you feeling conflicted and confused, but wanting more. Agents are magnetic and charming. They're easy to fall for because they love the good life, they like nice things, they're social, and they know how to have fun. Agents love being the center of attention (when their clients are not around, of course) and if they like you, they will make you feel like the most special person in the room. Expect him to wine and dine you with nice restaurants, great parties, and first-class service. He's persistent and romantic, and the more you resist, the more intrigued he'll become. Sadly, the minute you let him in, you'll realize that you can never get his undivided attention. This is not entirely his fault. Agents are already in a number of relationships. Their clients act like girlfriends; they call them constantly with every problem, from lack of self-esteem to wardrobe and relationship issues. Though he will continue to take you to the hottest restaurants in town, he will also get up numerous times during dinner to take a call, stroke a client's ego, or pitch a potential client who just happens to be sitting two tables away from you. Welcome to Hollywood, baby!

His Look

Fashion conscious, materialistic, professional, smooth. Agents always wear a suit and tie in the office. Higher-ups are decked out in Armani suits and Prada shoes, with the smallest and hippest cell phone to match. Expect all of these guys, regardless of rank, to have the newest and latest gadgets (stereo equipment, flat-screen TV, golf clubs, etc.), including a nice watch, and, if he lives in LA, a cool car. These guys work hard to appear powerful and connected; they need to have everything desirable before everyone else has it. In addition, they demand special treatment, so expect them to have free tickets to sporting events, concerts, even benefits. The more invitations they get, the more successful they feel.

His Vibe

Confident and comfortable in every situation, even when he's not. Agents are typically funny, animated, smooth, and social. They're also great storytellers and they know how to pick and choose their audience. Agents know how to work a room. They have a short attention span (yes, this may translate into an inability to settle down), and they hate to stay in one place for too long; they secretly fear they're missing out on other opportunities. Still, as social and magnetic as they seem, deep down they're often self-conscious, paranoid, and insecure. This is a backstabbing, vicious business, and agents will try anything to steal one another's clients. Don't be surprised if your guy does a lot of client name-dropping. He's not just being pretentious—remember, these guys are only as good as the people they represent.

His Hours

An agent's work is never done. Expect him to get calls from clients at any time of day or night, and that includes weekends. Call him during a workday and you'll get his assistant every time. Though she will give him the message, chances are he won't be able to get back to you. He is swamped with calls from clients, internal meetings, work lunches, you name it. At night he has drinks, dinners, award shows, and premieres scheduled weeks in advance. Remember, he needs to be out there networking for his existing clients and at the same time, looking for new ones. So what does this mean for you? You will be squeezed into his schedule, when there's a cancellation, of course. Weekends are spent reading scripts and novels, prescreening movies, and viewing pilot episodes of new TV shows, etc. If he's a TV agent, beware of pilot season (December through mid-May). This is his personal hell (and chances are it will be yours too). Pilot season is when all the new television shows get picked up and agents are busy trying to staff them. As for the film agents, expect them to entertain more than TV agents do. They also travel more, attending all the major film festivals and award shows (i.e., Sundance, Aspen Comedy Festival, and the Video Music Awards). Although he calls these "work" functions, there is definitely a little bit of playtime. Don't worry too much. He's probably too stressed to have any real fun.

Risk Factor

He's so used to being "on" for work, it makes it hard to know who he really is. He's also afraid to let down his guard with you (he's not used to being vulnerable), and even though he'll come on strong and make you feel like the most special person in the world (agents are known for that), instinctively he'll want to run when things get too serious. Expect him to be double-booked with drinks, dinners, screenings, and award shows. Yes, he'll be schmoozing with beautiful people (ahem, women) and when he's not out searching for new clients, he'll be busy taking care of existing ones, filling their every need no matter how ridiculous the request.

Perks

He knows how to get things done. He's well connected, animated, funny, fun, social, and spontaneous. You will never be bored. He's also a great negotiator—he can get you the best table at a restaurant and that handbag you wanted at a great discount. He likes nice things and he'll want you to have nice things too. Yes, he will make a good living, assuming he has good clients. And remember, image is everything in this business so chances are, you'll be living in a big house and driving a nice car.

The Assistant

Beware, she reads his e-mails!

Assistants have an entirely different demeanor than secretaries, and they are much more difficult to befriend. Unlike secretaries, assistants are typically young (most are fresh out of college), eager, and ambitious, and they will stop at nothing to get promoted (this includes kissing your boyfriend's butt). Assistants tend to work in the media and entertainment industry, and their job is meant to be a stepping stone, not a life-long career. As a result, they're fiercely loyal to their employers and most of them stay at work until their bosses have left for the day (unlike secretaries, who leave work at 5 P.M.). Carey, a fashion publicist whose last two boyfriends had female assistants says, "They don't care about your relationship, and they hate small talk. They have no qualms about canceling your dates, and you'll never get a reason out of them other than 'he's stuck in a meeting.' Also, they listen to their boss's voice mails and check his e-mails, so don't do anything embarrassing! If you have the urge to say something private, just picture that little twenty-two-year-old assistant sitting with your guy, laughing about you over lattes (made just the way he likes them). Don't reveal anything about your relationship. You're better off acting extremely confident and aloof. Show no weakness with her. And remember, you too are busy and have a life."

Who does he represent?

Though big-time actors, writers, athletes, and directors frequently shift from one agency to the next, here's a look at the top five places and who they currently represent:

- Endeavor:
  Paris Hilton, Jude Law, Mark Wahlberg
- Creative Artists Agency (CAA):
  Jennifer Aniston, Mischa Barton, Angelina Jolie
- United Talent Agency (UTA):
  Justin Timberlake, Wilmer Valderrama, Elizabeth Hurley
- William Morris Agency:
  Ray Romano, Eddie Murphy, Kelly Ripa
- International Creative Management (ICM):
  Jennifer Lopez, Britney Spears, Nick Lachey

Will You Rule Him Out?

Before you decide, here's a look at what to expect when you are dating a talent agent.

Rule #1:

He will talk on his cell phone, occasionally more than he talks to you.

His cell phone is his lifeline; his clients are his existence. Get used to listening to his work conversations everywhere you go. Chances are he'll spend entire car rides on his cell phone, which means you'll have to turn down the radio and zone out. Sometimes his calls are necessary; other times they're rude. Secretly these guys fear silence; they thrive on being needed and connected. Julie has gotten used to this: "I've been with my fiancé for two years and when we go out, he has his cell phone attached to his ear and he's checking his e-mail. If we go to a restaurant, his cell phone is on the table and usually I have to order for him because he's too busy on the phone to look at the menu. It's just how it is."

Rule #2:

He will expect his assistant to do everything for him. Make sure he doesn't expect that from you.

He will be in touch with his assistant at least twenty times a day telling her to do everything from pick up his dry cleaning to make reservations for your birthday dinner. His assistant knows more about his life than you do. She will check his voice mail and read his e-mails (beware!), and generally make him feel like he is God. Assistants are at their boss's beck and call;

they will feed his ego and make him feel as though he deserves to be waited on. Your boyfriend will ask her what she ordered him for lunch last week that he liked so much, where she bought his mother's birthday gift last year, and which side of his car the gas tank is on. According to Julie, "Agents involve their assistants in their romantic relationships much more than other guys do. Expect her to call you to find out where you want to go to dinner, what your frequent flyer number is; what your ring size is. There will be no boundaries unless you set them. You definitely lose a level of intimacy when you're dating an agent. Make sure he doesn't get too used to delegating the tasks that involve you."

Rule #3:
He'll have breakfast, lunch, and dinner meetings scheduled for the next four weeks.

He's out almost every night having drinks or dinner with someone in the industry. If he doesn't have plans, you should be concerned. Agents spend their nights at screenings, premieres, award shows, benefits, showcases, you name it. And lots of times they won't be able to bring a date. According to Julie, "Being in a relationship with an agent is a juggling act. When someone flakes on a plan he may try to fill it with another work meeting or he might use it to schedule a date with you. Don't take this personally; it's the only time he has."

Rule #4:
Beware of his compliments.

This guy is great at telling you exactly what you want to hear, whether it's how beautiful you are, how special you are, or how much he can't believe that he's met someone like you. He will say things like, "Where have you been all my life." And no matter how resistant you think you are, most likely you will fall for it, every time. Remember, his job is to make people feel good. He spends his days pumping his client's egos, making them feel like they are on top of the world. Though he could be genuine, he could also be working on automatic pilot. Pay attention to how he treats other women and see if he's using the same lines with them.

Rule #5:
He will make big promises and may not keep them.

Agents love to make promises even if they consciously know that they won't follow through. They love to fantasize about taking you on romantic trips, taking you to this person's wedding in Costa Rica or that person's summer home in Nantucket. And they might plan as far as six months in advance when the two of you have only been seeing each other for three weeks. It's a little aggressive at first but it's exciting, and if you're not careful, you will get your hopes up. "I think agents are in love with the idea of being in love," says Tracy. "They want to be swept off their feet, but they're so busy trying to sweep you off your feet, that they forget to ask themselves if they're actually falling in love. If I had a dime for every time an agent told me he was going to take me away on some romantic vacation and didn't do it, I would be so rich that I'd need an agent to represent me!"

Rule #6:
He may be secretly afraid that being in a relationship will ruin his career.

Most agents love the scene and those who don't are simply afraid that if they're not in it, they will be forgotten. These guys need to be in the know. That means they need to be out and about at as many premieres, restaurants, parties, and benefits as possible. And they can't be standing in the corner with you all night, either. Once he's there he has to be "on" and schmoozing with existing clients, potential clients, studio executives, managers, you name it. They simply must know all the players. Though most guys won't come out and say this until it's too late, they're petrified that "having a girlfriend" will prevent them from networking to their full capacity. If you're jealous or demanding of his time, chances are he will run.

Rule #7:
He won't want you to know that he is stressed.

He's used to being the magnetic carefree guy, the guy who can handle any problem, at any time, with total ease. The truth is, his job is so high-pressure and intense that underneath it all, he's probably a bit of a mess. Remember, he's only as good as the clients he represents and his clients are only happy if he's getting them good work and making them feel like they're being taken care of. This is a lot of pressure. The closer you become to your agent boyfriend, the more stressed he will appear. Sadly, this guy has trouble letting you in and so he will try to put on an act, even with you. The last thing he wants is to let down his guard and admit that he's not the powerhouse everyone believes him to be. Get him to confide in you and he'll do one of two things—propose or run like hell.

He Says . . .

We will entertain beautiful women but that doesn't mean we want to sleep with them.

"Give us the benefit of the doubt. Yes, we have dinners, lunches, and drinks with celebrities and beautiful women in particular, but that doesn't mean that we want to sleep with them. These are simply the people we represent. It's our job. My last girlfriend kept asking me questions about every woman I met, and to be honest, it just became a big turn off. You want your girl to be confident and to understand that sleeping with hot women is not your biggest priority. I'd rather secure an A-list client than sleep with one—any day of the week."—Eric

We can't talk to you on the phone while we're at work.

"We can barely find time to use the bathroom, so don't expect us to be able to elicit interesting responses to your daily happenings when you call us at the office. Chances are, we are in a meeting, heading to a meeting, getting out of a meeting, or just about to get yelled at at the exact minute you call. Understand that we might sound abrupt or distant, and we might even ask our assistant to take a message—even when we know it's you. This has nothing to do with you! My best advice, and what I wish all my ex-girlfriends would have realized, is just don't call your boyfriend at the office. If it's superimportant, then of course we will make ourselves available. But if it's just to say hi and tell us you love us, drop us an e-mail or something. Oh, and we love you too."—**Brian**

We like to be in control.

"We take care of our clients all day, so when we get home chances are we won't be able to relinquish control. Though we might tell you that we want you to take care of things at home because that's what we do all day at the office, chances are we won't really be able to let go. It's not that we don't trust you or your ability to get things done. It's just that we can't stomach being out of the loop; plus, we've become quite particular about our likes and dislikes now that we're agents. So, what should you do if your boyfriend tells you to take care of your next vacation? Make sure he means it. Otherwise, he might take one look at the itinerary and then change everything at the last minute."—**Scott**

She Says . . .

Beautiful women will kiss his butt.

"I don't care how secure you are, if he's hanging out with models all day, it's going to suck for you. I dated an agent who represented models. First of all, he dressed impeccably and he would always comment on what I wore. He always wanted me to be more fashion forward and he was very into women and their bodies—not in a sexual way (at least that's what he said) but more in an artsy way, like how their clothes would fit. Second, he was constantly taking his clients (AKA, models) to glamorous events, fashion shows, and photo shoots. Sure, he would invite me, but I'm five foot two! I honestly felt inadequate every day. Eventually, I had to go and pretend that I wasn't insecure (he told me insecurity is a turnoff). My advice? Get to know his clients. They are never as cool and beautiful as you build them up to be."—Lisa

Agents fight other people's battles.

"He will take abuse all day long from other agents at the office. He is constantly going to bat for his clients, fighting their battles. Agents are essentially celebrities by default. I have this theory that most agents were actually dorks in high school and this is their way to get revenge on the world. Still, they get treated terribly while working their way up the corporate ladder, which means they seriously have to want it so badly. Agents live in a constant state of paranoia. Hollywood is a shady business and these guys are trained to professionally screw one another over."—Rebecca

Don't believe everything he tells you.

"An agent's job is to make other people feel good. His biggest talent is that he boosts you up and creates hype around you so that everyone else will see what he sees, including you. How does this affect you? He's a professional schmoozer, and a seamless flirt. Be careful not to take his compliments and promises too seriously. He's not intentionally lying to you when he tells you how beautiful you are and that he can't wait to take you skiing in Aspen. At the moment, he believes what he is saying. It's just that he lives in the moment (the opposite of an investment banker) and it's almost second nature for him to get carried away with you. I think agents are like actors in the sense that they love to fall in love."—Robin

The Breakdown

Here's a look at the talent agent:

biggest turn on	He's animated, magnetic, social, and connected
biggest challenge	Getting his full attention; keeping him away from his cell phone
best way to get in touch	Cell phone; he's always on it
greatest perk	He knows how to get things done; he's very connected
best timing	There's no good time

Talking Shop

Here's a list of key words and phrases that will help you speak his language:

Floater: No, this person is not flaky or noncommittal. He's just trying to break into the business. A floater is a temporary assistant who fills in for assistants who are out sick or on vacation. Be careful what you reveal to a floater who picks up your boyfriend's office line. Floaters have no loyalty to you or your man.

Green light: The famous two words that every agent wants to hear. Getting the green light means that you've received confirmation that the development of a project has ended and production is about to begin.

Hype: Overzealous praise or advertising. Agents have an uncanny ability to create hype around anyone and anything, regardless of whether it's warranted. "The agent created so much *hype* around the film that even Halle Berry thought *Cat Woman* would be a good career move."

Pitch: To sell someone on something, whether it's a client, a script, an agent, or an idea. Agents are always pitching (selling) to someone. They pitch their clients to TV show runners for TV jobs, casting agents for films, commercials, plays, you name it. In fact, they are so used to pitching, that most likely they will pitch themselves to you.

Poach: To trespass on another's property in order to take game. Agents constantly poach other agents' clients. It is not uncommon for an agent to poach a big movie star and tell her all the reasons why she should leave her current agent and come sign with him. It's kind of like hitting on someone else's girlfriend.

Premiere: The first showing of a movie, in a specific city or worldwide. Chances are your agent boyfriend will be attending many of these. Don't freak out if he doesn't invite you. Many agents are not encouraged to invite a plus-one. They are supposed to be networking, not sitting on the sidelines with you.

Producer: The money man. A producer makes all the arrangements for funding and developing a studio deal to get the film into production and distribution.

Staffing season: A period of time when new television shows are staffed with actors, writers, directors, etc. This is an incredibly stressful time for TV agents, who are working their butts off to get jobs for their clients.

Turnaround: Not a sexual command. In fact, if a project goes into turnaround most likely your boyfriend will feel far from sexual. Turnaround is a word used to mean that the option on a project (i.e., a screenplay) has expired and the party holding that option has chosen not to renew it.

chapter 5 The Consultant

He's that clean-cut guy standing in line at the airport carrying his laptop computer and a small carry-on bag with his company logo on the front. He practically glides through the security line, taking off his shoes and whipping out his laptop with such grace, you'd think he's spent his entire life going in and out of airports. You're intrigued, but just as you're about to start a conversation, he disappears into the admirals' club for frequent flyers. You wait impatiently at the gate, checking your boarding pass every five minutes, hoping that you have enough water, gum, and magazines to last you through the flight. And just when you think your new dream guy isn't going to make his flight, he casually reappears just in time to preboard with the rest of first class. So, who is this gold status guy and why hasn't he even noticed you? Most likely this has nothing to do with you and everything to do with the fact that he is in work mode. Consultants are constantly traveling and so they've had to learn how to maximize their time while they're en route. In fact, most of these guys spend the entire flight prepping for their next meeting.

His Look

Versatile and accommodating, consultants know a little bit about everything. They have a knack for blending into unfamiliar territory and making themselves and others feel at ease. So, what does this mean for you? He has every look in his closet from urban cowboy to street chic and, of course, your typical suit and tie, complete with cell phone holster. The problem? It's hard to tell which look is the real him.

His Vibe

Well spoken, analytical, and independent. These guys are confident and comfortable, regardless of their surroundings. They thrive on entering struggling companies and taking over. Some might say they like to play hero. Expect this guy to talk a lot. Even the simplest question will evoke a long-winded answer complete with hand gestures and consultant terminology. He may seem impressive at first: he's knowledgeable, charming, and well mannered, but ask yourself if you really understand what he's saying. Consultants have their own way of speaking and it's incredibly vague and ambiguous. Note: His job title is ambiguous, and so is the field. The truth is that anyone can call themselves consultants, so make sure you know what this guy is consulting on (i.e., management, accounting, software, real estate) and where he works. Is he an independent consultant (AKA, a freelancer who uses the term consultant to make himself sound more important than he is) or does he work for one of the top consulting firms (i.e., McKinsey, Bain, Gartner).

His Hours

This guy rarely works weekends and unless he's traveling, chances are he'll get home in time to have dinner with you. Good days start at 9 A.M. and end by 5:30 P.M. Still, consultants work on a project by project basis, so hours vary depending on the client he's working for. Slow times occur before each project begins, when consultants are waiting for a deal to be sold. This makes it incredibly difficult to make plans, especially if it's around holidays or birthdays. Unfortunately many projects involve travel, in remote areas, for weeks, sometimes months, at a time. If you're dating a consultant and he's not traveling, you should worry. His most stressful times are usually once a project begins or just before a "go-live," which is when the systems that they've been working on are put into effect. Note: Those who join consulting firms straight out of college are called analysts. Analysts typically spend two or three years at a consulting firm before returning to school to get an MBA, or abandoning the field of consulting altogether.

Risk Factor

He's constantly traveling, working with new teams filled with young people. Work romances or "convenient arrangements" are not uncommon, especially on the road. Though these guys don't have many plus-one perks, they do have plenty of expensed events with other coworkers including golf, long lunches, happy hours, steak houses, cigars, strip clubs, etc. Also, most consultants don't know exactly what they want to do with their lives, which is why they went into consulting to begin with (to get a taste of what's out there). Consultants are known to be "jacks-of-all-trades, masters of none." Don't be surprised if he bounces from one consulting firm to the next until he decides where he wants to be, or if he's committed to this field.

Perks

He's patient, organized, curious, and detail-oriented. He has a tremendous knowledge of how the business world works, and he's been exposed to a number of companies and how they operate. He's also a great problem solver, which means that (yes!) he'll listen to your problems and spend hours trying to find solutions. Consultants are curious, project-oriented, resourceful, and determined. Chances are he'll fix your DVD player, program your cell phone, and stay on the line with customer service for hours just to install your latest software. Also, expect him to have plenty of frequent flyer miles!

Top Five Most Prestigious Consulting Firms

- **McKinsey & Company:** Elite and powerful, the company offers plenty of perks, including free tickets to sporting events, monthly social events, first-class airline tickets, and a personal assistant, not to mention huge bonuses. Clients include Pepsi, IBM, and General Motors.
- **Boston Consulting Group:** Heavy travel (most clients are not located in Boston) is a part of working for this company. Still, Boston Consulting Group stresses a collaborative work environment (there is little competition) and a healthy work-life balance.
- **Bain & Company:** This firm has an entrepreneurial environment with a work hard, play hard mentality. Bain has a very collegiate feel. Clients include Staples, Dominos Pizza, and KB Toys.

- **Booz Allen Hamilton:** Conservative and a bit old-fashioned, this firm is a bit too stuffy according to some people. Though the salaries tend to be lower than other top-tier consulting firms, they are known for giving substantial bonuses.
- **Gartner:** With a laid-back and independent atmosphere, Gartner allows its employees to work from home if they prefer (huge plus!). In addition, they offer a one-month sabbatical after five years with the company. Did somebody say extended honeymoon?

Will You Rule Him Out?

Before you decide, here's a look at what to expect when you are dating a consultant.

Rule #1:
He will travel often.

Consultants are at the beck and call of their clients and at any moment they could be put on a new project (projects are also referred to as *engagements*) and sent off to spend weeks, maybe even months in a new city. Unfortunately they have little control over this and much of the time they don't even know how long they'll be gone. This is not his fault. It's just the nature of the business. And as much as it sucks, he needs you to understand this if you two are going to have a future together. "My boyfriend recently found out that he'd be leaving for Manchester, England, on Valentine's Day," says Jessica. "We had reservations at this great restaurant that I'd wanted to go to for months. When we knew he would have to leave for work, I changed our reservation to the following Wednesday, which was my birthday. Unfortunately he couldn't make it back in time for that either. It's disappointing, but there's nothing I can do about it and I know it's not his fault."

Rule #2:
Consultants won't know how to give you a straight answer.

Consultants have their own language (they call it *consultant speak*), which is basically a complicated way of answering questions and solving problems. Though they may think it sounds normal, the rest of the world has no clue what these guys are talking about, not to mention why it takes them an extra fifteen minutes (filled with ambiguous terminology) to answer a simple question. Chances are you'll be so confused by your boyfriend's response that by the time he's finished talking, you'll completely forget what you asked him in the first place! This can be incredibly frustrating, especially when you're trying to have the "relationship talk." Unfortunately, consultants have been trained to speak this way from the moment they entered the field. So what's this about? According to Patrick, "This language has been passed down from generation to generation. Let me put it simply," he says. "The metaphors and made-up technical words are a must. Basically, you must leverage the collaboration of numerous methodologies and processes to track the best practices of generating key terminology that is utilized in the professional services." Right, now do you ladies get what I am saying?

Rule #3:

Consultants are far from impulsive.

These guys are strategic thinkers and they like to have a well-thought-out plan of action before making any decisions. Expect your guy to come to the table with a full-blown timetable complete with a list of action items, subcategories, responsibilities, and future objectives. Though this might feel tedious at times, the good news is that you know he won't take off one morning and blow his savings on some sports car, or even worse, make impulsive decisions about the status of your relationship (typical Wall Street trader behavior). If a consultant wants to break up with you, chances are he's got a whole spreadsheet filled with reasons why. Ask him, and he just might pull it out for you.

Rule #4:
Consultants are incredibly adaptable.

Consultants are accustomed to entering unfamiliar territory (i.e., companies) and making themselves feel right at home. Their job is literally to come into their client's space (even though they may know nothing about it) and create new systems and solutions to help the company operate more efficiently. These guys spend weeks, sometimes months, at a time living in remote towns, working in new office spaces with new people. Some might say that consultants thrive on change and find it challenging to work in new and different environments. These guys rarely work in their own office, which means that they're quite comfortable entering other people's space and taking over. Beware of his sense of boundaries. Many consultants don't know what it feels like to have others intrude on them and so they don't realize that their actions might feel a bit aggressive. The good news is that these guys are not set in their ways. In fact, with the exception of the struggling artist (who prefers your apartment because it's nicer than his hole in the wall), the consultant might be the only guy who actually enjoys sleeping at your apartment.

Rule #5:
He will need to micromanage everything.

It's extremely difficult for consultants to sit back and let others manage a project, especially when they feel they can manage the task in a more efficient manner. According to Heidi, you should get ready to have him take over your entire wedding: "People used to tell me that the guys don't get involved in the wedding plans, but with Patrick it was the opposite. When we met with the wedding coordinator, he pulled out a huge spreadsheet of tasks and deadlines and a timeline of the wedding reception in fifteen-minute intervals! There were three copies—one for me, one for him, one for the wedding coordinator. I'll never forget the look on her face when she saw that spreadsheet."

He Says . . .

Find out when his weekly status calls are.

"You should know when your guy is 'out of pocket,' which means he's not accessible. Every consultant has a weekly status meeting, which could last hours. Know when this is and plan accordingly. Also, know when his most stressful times are. Most consultants have three stressful times in their schedule. First, when we start a new project and we are in a new environment with a new client. Yes, we're adaptable creatures but we're still trying to find our way and that can be stressful. Second, we get stressed at the end of each project when the actual solution or application we've been working on goes into effect. This is called a *go-live,* and it's when we get to test out the applications and make sure everything we've done is actually working properly. And finally, we get stressed when we are changing jobs. There's a lot of turnover in this business and consultants tend to change jobs every two to three years."—Patrick

We don't want to leave you.

"Yes, we chose this traveling lifestyle, but most likely we did it before we met you, and now we hate that we have to keep leaving every time things start to feel normal. Still, this is our life and in some ways travel can spice up a relationship. You get to miss each other, plan for our return, and spend time with your friends. . . . Just don't concoct this whole thing in your head that the guy is leaving town to get away from you. We're not asking to be put on certain projects. It just happens that travel is a big component of any consultant's job."—AJ

She Says . . .

The worst thing you can do is fight when he's away.

"My boyfriend spent four months living in London for a last-minute project. They gave him one week's notice and he had to pack up his bags and move. That's the worst part, that they don't give you any notice. We were about to get engaged, which made it so much worse. I was so angry and he would call and tell me he missed me, but still I couldn't deal with the fact that he was going to be gone for so long. We fought a lot on the phone, which sucked. And the six-hour time change made things even worse. Eventually we got used to being away from each other, which isn't the best solution, but it got us through."—Mackenzie

The Breakdown

Here's the lowdown on the consultant:

biggest turn on	He likes to fix things
biggest challenge	Explaining what he does for a living
best way to get in touch	His cell phone, which is most likely attached to his belt
greatest perk	Frequent flyer miles
best timing	When he's in between projects

Talking Shop

Here's a list of key words and phrases that will help you speak his language:

The beach: No, it's not where he's taking you on your first date. The beach refers to the free time a consultant has between client projects. This is a great time to meet this guy because he's relatively stress free and available to focus on you.

Behind the eight ball: A phrase he'll use to describe that it's crunch time. When he's behind the eight ball it means that he's up against a deadline. This means he will probably be stressed and might even need some space to get things done.

Boondoggle: A "business trip" that involves very little actual work (maybe it's a seminar or a conference) in an exotic location, like Hawaii. Boondoggles are far from stressful and often include lots of relaxing and partying. Hopefully your boyfriend will take you on one of these.

Engagements: Don't run off to Tiffany's just yet. Engagements is a term consultants use to define various client projects, not the status of your relationship. Engagements can last anywhere from a couple of weeks to several years.

Expense report: A documented list of expenses this guy has incurred while traveling or entertaining clients. Note: Help him fill out his expense reports. It's a great way to see what he's been up to on all those business trips!

Go-live: Signifies the end of a project. A "go-live" is when the new systems that consultants have put in place (all this time that he's been working on a certain project) are tested. This is one of his most stressful times, so go easy on him.

Loop back around: Another consulting term, which means to check back with you and keep you abreast of the status of a certain task. "Once I've spoken with the client, I will loop back around with you to discuss next steps."

Out of pocket: A phrase consultants used to imply that they'll be unreachable. "I'll be out of pocket for the next forty-five minutes." Just make sure he's not "out of pocket" for the majority of your relationship.

Pull-up: No, we're not talking about the biceps exercise. A pull-up is a meeting to share and evaluate findings and set direction for work going forward. It's possible that your consultant boyfriend could be "out of pocket" for a "pull-up."

Put out fires: Sorry to burst your bubble, but this guy is not literally running into burning buildings to save lives, although he will act like the work he is doing is almost that important. When consultants talk about "putting out fires," they're talking about running damage control and cleaning up other people's screwups.

Status call: Beware of the weekly status call, because it could last for hours. The status call is typically a conference call with the client to discuss what's been done and what needs to be completed. Consultants have a number of status calls, and it's important to find out when these are so that you don't disturb him.

chapter 6 The Entrepreneur

There's something incredibly sexy about this guy. He's a risk taker, a doer, and his very own boss. If you stick by him, you are in for the ride of your life. For your first date, he meets you for drinks at some posh, hard-to-get-into hot spot (entrepreneurs love to be in the know). By his second Jack and Coke, he's pitching you his new business venture. His excitement is thrilling, so much so that you feel like you're part of something huge, with lots of financial reward! Sure, you feel a little short-shrifted that he barely noticed your low-cut dress, but he seems so powerful and creative and passionate that it almost doesn't matter.

When he walks you home and kisses you good night, he promises to let you know if tomorrow's meeting to "get financing" goes well. You fall asleep smiling. You feel like you are a part of something big. Maybe you'll go into business with your new entrepreneurial boyfriend, developing new ideas over breakfast and selling them at dinner. That is, of course, if he succeeds.

His Look

He has a few of them. If he's just started his entrepreneurial venture, don't expect him to have an office. Chances are he's sitting at home in his pajamas writing business plans and setting up meetings. This means no shirt, no shoes, just boxers. If he's been at this for a while, he may have a small office with one or two people working with him or for him. Usually this means he's settled into the corporate casual look: pants (slacks or jeans) and a button-down. Those who are off at meetings with potential clients, or banks to get funding, will most likely break out their best suits and briefcases from the days when, ahem, they had a desk job.

His Vibe

This guy is passionate, enthusiastic, and incredibly self-involved. Work dictates his life and his mood, so expect him to appear manic at times. He will be either incredibly high and confident or incredibly low and vulnerable. Some days he will want to talk about his work for hours, other days not at all. Don't probe too much if he doesn't want to talk. An entrepreneur walks a fine line between failure and success every day.

His Hours

Never-ending, especially in the beginning when he's trying to get his company off the ground. An entrepreneur never leaves work at his office, even when he actually has one. If he's not completely obsessed with his work, you should worry. In order to be a successful entrepreneur, he needs to be thinking about work almost all the time. Remember, he's his own boss, which means that he's responsible for the success or failure of the company. Note: Only one out of ten small businesses actually succeeds.

Risk Factor

Financial risks, endless hours, and emotional ups and downs. Make sure this guy is actually capable of starting and running his own business. Some guys become entrepreneurs by default, because they can't keep a job or they don't like having a boss to tell them what to do. Find out his track record and see if he has a backup plan. Regardless of whether he will be a success, most entrepreneurs are obsessed with their work and most of them view a relationship as an additional responsibility. Don't smother him and don't freak out if he doesn't answer your phone calls all day. It's because he's engrossed in his work (or he just went bankrupt), not because he's sleeping with someone else.

Perks

He's adventurous, motivated, and incredibly passionate (all major turn ons!), plus he's not the kind of guy who's willing to settle in life. Entrepreneurs are some of the most exciting, creative people you'll meet. Date this guy and you'll never be bored. Who knows, he might hit the jackpot!

Will You Rule Him Out?

Before you decide, here's a look at what to expect when you are dating an entrepreneur.

Rule #1:

Your life together is on hold until his business gets off the ground.

Get used to a lack of stability. If this guy's a young entrepreneur just starting out, most likely he has very little money coming in, and even though he might make tons of it down the line, right now you're banking on his potential. Though this can be incredibly exciting, it can also be exhausting. "I had complete faith in him. It wasn't a matter of whether or not he would succeed, which eventually he did. It was just that we both wanted stability," says Lindsey. "We'd been living without an income from him for so long that we desperately wanted to get to a point where there was some money coming in."

For Carly, it wasn't that simple: "It's impossible to plan a future with a guy while he is trying to get his business off the ground, especially if the business takes years of planning. I thought the whole entrepreneurial thing was exciting at first, but after two years it started to feel really unrealistic. I was always waiting for something to happen so that our life could begin. We talked about moving in together and getting engaged, and yet we couldn't because he was always waiting for someone to buy his company or at least invest in it. He said he wanted to be at a certain stage with his career before he got engaged, but he never got there. Eventually, we broke things off. And I was resentful because I put so much of my life into his venture only to realize that it wasn't taking off and neither were we."

Rule #2:
True entrepreneurs don't approach things half-assed.

If you're dating an entrepreneur who doesn't live and breathe his new venture, get out of the relationship! Though you may enjoy all the time he spends with you because he's available in the middle of the day, if he doesn't get his business off the ground, chances are your relationship won't make it off the ground either. Tara dated a "half-assed" entrepreneur for nine months before his business folded and he went crawling back to his hometown: "Don't kid yourself. If I had paid attention earlier, I would have realized that he wasn't working hard enough to make the business work. Deep down I knew that he was more caught up in the glamorous side of his new fashion company than he was in the intricate details. He'd sleep late, take long 'networking' lunches with designers and models, and stay out at social cocktail parties until 3 in the morning. He always invited me to go, but I wasn't all that interested in hanging out with a bunch of models and being 'fabulous.' He said all the socializing was essential to promoting his new business, which was true; he did get a lot of press. Still, the whole business flopped after a year, and that's when he packed up his stuff and moved back home."

Rule #3:
He will talk about work all the time.

He will be incredibly passionate about his business and every intricate detail, so don't be surprised if he wants to share his excitement with you—and everyone else who happens to be around. Though this may become tedious after a while, it's actually better than the alternative, which is shutting you out. Still, if you can, try to get him to reach some sort of happy medium; otherwise he's going to drive you insane. "At the very beginning stages I was really supportive and involved, and we would talk about his new restaurant constantly, but then after a few months it kind of got to be annoying because it felt like that was *all* we talked about," says Lindsey. "If it wasn't one thing that he was stressed about it was another. From hiring a general contractor, to picking out plates, to choosing a menu item . . . everything was a major decision in his mind, whereas some of those things began to seem me trivial to me. The cell phone thing got to be sort of an argument trigger point for us also. He was always getting calls and very often we'd be sitting in a small restaurant trying to enjoy dinner and he'd be on the phone discussing everything and anything loud enough for anyone to hear. It's hard to get them to realize that as much as you love and support them, they need to focus a little time on you too. In the end though, I'd rather have a passionate creative guy than a guy who hates his work and comes home and complains about it."

Rule #4:

The true entrepreneur will work insane hours to get his business off the ground.

Remember, this guy is his very own boss, which means that when he's not working, no one is—unless he's hired a staff. Still, this business venture is most likely his baby, and he will treat it with the same passion that an artist treats his paintings, poems, songs, etc. Expect him to work throughout the weekends without even questioning whether he should really be at the office on a Saturday night. The good news is that he's his own boss, which means that he should be able to take your calls and find time to have dinner with you. The bad news is that he is responsible for everything that could go wrong, so he is constantly preoccupied. "Yes, we had breakfast and dinner together, but only if I came down to his office, and even then he was taking calls throughout our meals," says Stephanie. "There were times that I felt like I was single again without the fun of going out or dating. You have to be incredibly independent to make it through those last few months before his business launches. It might sound pathetic, but I had to start getting creative with how I would entertain myself. I learned how to knit, I did a lot of crossword puzzles, I had a lot of time to catch up with friends, and I also cooked a lot. I would try new recipes and make elaborate meals for myself—anything to stay occupied at night."

Rule #5:
An entrepreneur is always looking for new opportunities.

This guy is a risk taker and a doer. He's always looking for the next best thing; even if he's launched a successful new business, he still wants more. Expect him to be on to the next thing the minute his work seems to calm down. Entrepreneurs thrive on the fast-paced environment and new opportunities. Plus, they like to make money. So, don't be surprised if he ends up selling his first business, which he slaved over, only to invest his profits into a new venture. Remember, it's rare for an entrepreneur to settle down, ever. What does this mean for you? It means that dating an entrepreneur is a way of life and you need to make sure that you can deal with that. This guy thrives on the unknown and the possibility of great things. He can never settle down completely, at least not in his work life. So, just because you made it through one business venture with him doesn't mean that it's smooth sailing from here on out. Instead, it means welcome to round two. The good news? You will never be bored.

Rule #6:
He will have a hard time letting go of his work, even for a weekend.

Looking forward to your vacation time? Don't get your hopes up. This guy will have a hard time letting go, at least those first few years. "My boyfriend wasn't able to go away at all. We had a few weddings that I had to go to alone, and I ended up taking two trips home to see my family because I was tired of being alone on the weekends," says Erica. "I remember the hardest time was when I had a coworker's wedding to go to and everyone was bringing their boyfriends except for me. My boyfriend had been working crazy hours for about three months and I was just really tired of it all. I had become very distant in an attempt to not be a whiny girlfriend, but in order to do that, I had to shut down. I had to force myself to not need anything from him. So that night it was the most gorgeous wedding and everyone just seemed so in love, and it made me feel that much more alone. It can be very difficult at times."

He Says . . .

Be supportive.

"I know so many guys that wouldn't even think of settling down with a woman when they are trying to get their business off the ground, but I think it depends on the woman. She has to be patient and supportive, someone who shares our enthusiasm for what we do and will understand the insane sacrifices that we make to follow our dreams. If a guy has a girlfriend like that (which I am lucky enough to have), then trust me, he won't go anywhere. If anything he will be that much more in love with her because he knows how much she believes in him."—Matt

Take an interest in his projects.

"True entrepreneurs are always thinking about their company and ways to improve it, and we always want to talk about it. It's my favorite subject, and it never gets old. The best girlfriends are the ones that let us share our excitement as well as our frustration."—Mark

Make sure you believe in him.

"We need your support and confidence. We need a woman who'll give us confidence when we're feeling beat down, when shit is not going our way on a particular day. The last thing we can handle is your feelings of doubt. Ask yourself if you even want to be with an entrepreneur, because it takes a certain personality to be able to deal with the entrepreneurial lifestyle. I dated a woman for two years and it was amazing while I was in business school, but the minute I graduated and started my own company, she was petrified. She thought I would work for a big company and live a stable, secure existence, but that just wasn't my dream. It was obvious that we had two entirely different outlooks on life."—Eric

She Says . . .

Get involved in his projects.

"Try to put yourself in his shoes and get involved. Help him make decisions so that you can have a sense of pride in the final result. If you don't care about this thing he is devoting *all* his time to, then you are really going to get bitter. At the same time, know what your boundaries are. A lot of people (close friends and family) had a lot of opinions and criticisms about the small details of my boyfriend's new venture, so I tried not to be like that even when I saw him do things that I would have done differently."—Jodi

Expect him to be moody at times.

"The hardest thing to understand is that even though it's his baby and he is totally consumed by whatever it is he is doing, he still might be miserable during certain phases of the project. It's like here you are giving this guy everything you have so that he can chase his dreams and be happy, and even though he's totally consumed, he's also totally exhausted and miserable. My only advice is to be patient. A lot of times he is learning as he goes, and eventually he will learn how to manage his time. It took my boyfriend a few months to realize that he needed to hire a manager to open and close the restaurant. Now he's much less stressed and more pleasant to be around."—Tara

Get used to living big.

"Entrepreneurs are larger than life and they exude an incredible energy and confidence, which makes everyone else want to be around them. These guys like the good life—they work hard and they play hard—and they surround themselves with people who are also living it up. They're social, intelligent, energetic, and charming. A true entrepreneur will never stop thinking of ways to raise money and make things happen. He will also never choose to get that extra hour of sleep. This guy's number one love is life, and its endless possibilities. Though he may travel often, which isn't so bad for a relationship because you get to miss each other, most likely he will bring you back great gifts! Marry an entrepreneur and you'll never be bored."—Chloe

The Breakdown

Here's the skinny on the entrepreneur:

biggest turn on	He's passionate and creative
biggest challenge	Success
best way to get in touch	His cell phone
greatest perk	He's excited about his work
best timing	After he's sold his first company

part 2: The Artists

"The first gift given to me in my relationship with a businessman was a Prada bag, because he thought I should have one. The first gift given to me from my musician boyfriend was a practice drum pad, because during one of our first conversations I mentioned that one day I'd like to play drums." —Alison

The artist is a passionate, creative, sensitive soul. Though his first love will always be his craft, he will still be one of the most romantic, spontaneous, and intuitive individuals you will ever meet. Artists thrive on raw emotion and inspiration. As a result, they fall in love easily, and without fear. They would rather risk everything to experience the ups and downs of life than to sit safely on the sidelines as an observer. Unlike bankers and lawyers, artists are extremely passionate about what they do. And what could be sexier than that? Unfortunately, as inspiring as they are, they can also be extremely self-absorbed and moody. Their work is an extension of who they are and as a result, many of them feel more fulfilled by work than they do by anything else.

the lowdown

his job	personality traits	most commonly used gadget	how he spends his weekends	his biggest concern	his busiest time
actor	self-absorbed, passionate, moody	cell phone	at the gym	getting his big break	end of a project
musician	creative, passionate, emotional	musical instrument	rehearsing	signing a record deal	touring
writer	quirky, witty, intimate	computer	writing	making a living	just before a deadline

chapter 7 The Actor

He's scruffy, adorable, and far from what you thought you'd end up with. But when he smiles, you melt. All of your friends are searching for stability, the suit, the dad-in-training. You are looking for LOVE. You blow him a kiss from the other side of the bar and he shoots you a devilish smile from behind his bartending station. Yes, he's a bartender, for the moment, but you know he'll get his big break—and when he does, you'll be right there playing his leading lady. Your parents think you're crazy, and your friends thought so too, until they got a good look at him. For some reason you don't care. You feel more alive than ever, like you're really living life with someone who puts himself on the line each and every day. And while everyone else is coming home exhausted from eighteen-hour days, your guy appears invigorated and ready to take the world by storm. Sounds nice, right? While it might make for a great short film, the unedited version could be anything but Oscar-worthy.

His Look

He cares about it, a lot. Don't be surprised to find him standing in front of your mirror, wondering if he's retaining water or losing hair. Actors, regardless of how sweet, are self-absorbed and vain—yes, he has more beauty products than you do. But hey, looking good is a big part of his job description. As for his clothes, most actors dress casual, but stylish (Paper Denim jeans, a worn-out but perfectly fitted T-shirt, scuffed-up shoes, and cool sunglasses). His look is much more about maintaining an image than it is about showing off a bunch of labels.

His Vibe

Confident and generous one minute, insecure and selfish the next. Actors are emotional, passionate, particular, impulsive, and moody. He is used to being coddled, whether it's by his agent, manager, or publicist (telling him how great he is). Actors get used to being the center of attention. When they're not, things become difficult.

His Hours

They depend on the genre. TV actors have relatively predictable hours (drama actors work longer hours than sitcom actors), whereas screen actors, even extras, might disappear for months to shoot a picture in the Far East. As for the struggling actor, he's most likely picking up shifts at the local bar between auditions. The good news is that you can always visit him for free drinks.

Risk Factor

He's mentally all over the place. If you like structure and stability, this is not the guy for you. He's notorious for losing track of time, whether that means completely blanking on your date (leaving you sitting in the restaurant by yourself), letting his cell phone battery die for hours, or even worse, disappearing for weeks only to follow up with a "hey baby" phone call that leaves you completely confused. Besides that, your biggest concerns are his on-camera love scenes (which suck regardless of how secure you are), last-minute travel plans (especially when you're not invited), female fans, and an unpredictable salary. He could make tons of cash, but he could also be close to broke. Remember, there are plenty of working actors who don't walk the red carpet, unless there happens to be one leading to their fifth-floor walkup.

Perks

They could be as fabulous as movie premiere tickets, private planes, five-star accommodations, and award shows, or as painful as front-row seats to his three-hour independent production of *Othello*.

Will You Rule Him Out?

Before you decide, here's a look at what to expect when you're dating an actor.

Rule #1:

All actors are selfish.

Why do you think they became actors to begin with? They love the spotlight. Even the nice, thoughtful ones put themselves first; it's part of the job. Sure, his acting dream started with some innocent high school play or a touching production for underprivileged children, but now it's way more serious than that. Acting is a demanding craft. When performing, actors must inhabit the characters they play, feeling what they feel and thinking how they think, which is very personal, emotional work. Then, when out and about in the real world, actors must always be cognizant of their appearance and behavior, lest a picture of them in big sunglasses and sweatpants ends up on the cover of *Star* magazine. Remember this when it seems like the only thing he's concerned about is which parts he'll lose now that he's got a receding hairline. Is it his fault that he's self-absorbed? Not really. Sure, actors are put on pedestals and given special treatment wherever they go. However, this celebrity comes at a very high price.

Rule #2:

Actors have a short attention span and get bored quickly.

Actors are always looking for the next best thing, their big break. This guy loves the chase, and the possibility, and he will work hard to win you over. He's also charming and magnetic, and he will make you feel like the most special woman in the world. He'll tell you that you're amazing. Yes, he will use the word *amazing.* At first you'll be shy. After all, how could he fall for you so quickly? But then you'll let down your guard and tell him that you're crazy about him too. And once you do, he'll run like hell. Why? He's actually much better at the courting thing than he is at the relationship. Sadly, he can't handle the responsibility, and he fears that spending too much time with you will take time away from networking with the *right* people. This change of heart will usually occur at the first sign you're having a relationship issue. Maybe you want something from him; maybe you need something from him. Whatever it is, he simply can't handle it and so he disappears. His most likely excuse: *I just can't handle a relationship right now. I have to focus on me.*

Rule #3:
He will disappear for days, sometimes weeks, and then reappear as if nothing's happened.

He has no concept of time. He has no set schedule. Instead, his schedule is dictated by what his agent and manager tell him to do, and when no one's telling him what to do he just sort of "hangs out" like a high school kid during lunch hour. He's also very caught up with himself. He's not trying to be rude, he just can't think about life from anyone else's perspective, unless he is trying to get into character, and even then he won't make the connection. Don't be surprised if he spends every night with you for two whole weeks and then forgets to tell you that he's taking off to shoot a movie in the Far East. Actors fall in and out of love quickly, depending upon their schedule. So, if you meet when he's in between projects, make sure you find out what it will be like when his schedule gets crazy. Though he might disappear for weeks, leaving you with a broken heart, chances are he will resurface the next time he's in town. The overly confident working actors are known to check back weeks, sometimes months later, as if no time has gone by. This can be incredibly disruptive if you don't have much going on in your life or you haven't gotten over him.

So, how do you deal with this? Angela spent two years on again, off again with her actor boyfriend and she says, "You have to develop a thick skin and act as if you didn't notice that he left town. That's the only way it won't bother you." Heather, another ex-girlfriend says, "I've dated a few guys who disappeared to shoot a film and then months later they called when they were back in town. And they had no idea that they did anything wrong." According to Joanna, a celebrity stylist, "You have to let him know in the beginning of your relationship that you're not going to stand for any actor bullshit. Teach him to use the phone and get him a watch! It's the oddest thing, but actors have no concept of time. They'll call you at 7 A.M. or 11 P.M. and it doesn't even cross their mind that you might be sleeping. They're just like, 'Hey, what's up baby?' as if you're just hanging out with your friends waiting for someone to call."

Rule #4:
Actors have a fear of commitment.

They don't like responsibility unless it's connected to furthering their career. When he is feeling added pressure, he will disappear. He doesn't want to be responsible for your happiness when he can't even get a handle on his own. He also doesn't want to tie himself down because so much of his job is about being at the right place at the right time, and unless he is incredibly confident in his career, he will secretly fear that he is missing out on career opportunities by sitting at home watching *American Idol* with you.

Rule #5:
He will walk all over you if you let him.

Don't let him. Actors get used to being put on a pedestal, and they can usually get away with everything, including blowing you off one night and then making it up to you the next night. Sadly, we put up with it because, well, they are hot, and famous. Jenna admits that she got carried away when a well-known, handsome actor hit on her in Los Angeles: "Yes, I ended up spending the night with him, and yes, it was amazing—or so I thought. But when I woke up the next morning he was putting on his jeans and zipping up his suitcase. He even let the bellman come in to take his bags! Sure, he said goodbye. He even told me he had a great time. Then he told me to leave my number with the concierge so that he could call me again when he got back in town!"

Rule #6:
Actors don't like to be alone.

They are so used to being surrounded by agents, directors, writers, etc., that it can get lonely when these people disappear. So, don't be surprised if your actor hookup calls you completely sober at 2 A.M. to tell you that he's just sitting by himself and watching TV and that he'd love some company. Though he's not drunk, this is still a booty call.

Rule #7:
He's not as confident as he looks.

Actors are used to being the center of attention. When they're not, things can become difficult. "I dated an actor for a few months and I noticed that whenever we went out to dinner and he wasn't the center of attention, he would get aggravated. He used to play this little joke where he'd knock over his glass of water at the table and make everyone jump out of their seats to avoid being soaked," says Rachel. "He thought it was hysterical, but it was actually pretty embarrassing and childish." Don't be surprised if he has trouble making his own decisions either. Actors are used to being taken care of, whether it's by their publicist, agent, manager, stylist, or girlfriend.

Likely Cast of Characters

Rolling out the red carpet? Before you do, here's a look at your potential plus-ones:

- **The struggling actor (AKA, your most likely candidate):** This guy spends his days attending casting calls, sending out head shots, running lines, performing in tiny theaters, and watching reruns on your couch. His schedule is that he doesn't have one. Possible perk: Most of these guys (except for the trust fund babies) double as bartenders, which could mean free drinks and access to some of the biggest hot spots.
- **The voice-over guy:** Though he might make great money if he's on-air a lot (every time his commercial airs he gets a percentage), most likely he's not following his passion. He tells himself (and you) that he is an actor, but he's doing commercials to make extra cash. While this may be true, the more comfortable he gets in this genre, the more difficult it is to break out. Just look at the Verizon guy. Could you ever imagine him in a serious drama?
- **The sitcom actor:** He has a surprisingly normal schedule and assuming he's got the gig and the show isn't being canceled, his job is relatively

stable. He shows up at the studio every morning and spends the day either running lines with the cast and crew or taping episodes.

- **The TV drama actor:** One-hour shows mean more lines to learn and longer rehearsals, plus the challenge of filming on location. His hours will vary depending on where the cameras are shooting that day and whether the producers need to film in the early mornings, late nights, or at the brink of nightfall.
- **The movie star:** Unless he's scheduled to film in your hometown, you might want to rethink this relationship. Dating an onscreen actor takes a lot of trust, and if you don't trust him, then get out! The last thing you want is to question him every time he shoots a love scene.

He Says . . .

We lose track of time.

"I've been reamed on this a thousand times. I'll tell a woman that I'll call her later and then I don't end up calling until the next day. It's terrible, I know, but when we're in rehearsals or shooting a movie, we're completely focused on running lines or working with the cast and crew. We are always trying to get somewhere, get noticed, move into a bigger role . . . it's hard to convince yourself to sit back and enjoy where you are. Plus, in our defense, we can't have our cell phones on set while we are shooting and there's no way to know how long it's going to take to shoot our scene."—Jason

We have to be focused on ourselves.

"People think that we're so self-absorbed, but when you think about it, we don't have much of a choice. We are basically our own business. Also, there is a lot of pressure to prove everyone else wrong. People always want to know what play you are in or what project you are working on. It's always this fine line between whether you've made it or you haven't. It can be exhausting."—Jacob

It's not a phase!

"Some women want to think that we'll get tired of the whole acting thing and become a suit. Trust me; unless a guy tells you otherwise, chances are he's trying to make a career out of this. We always get the bad rap for being the players who date all these different women, but what about the women who dump us the minute they get tired of struggling? If I had a dollar for every time a girlfriend of mine said, 'I just want to be able to live nicely,' I wouldn't be having this conversation."—Eddie

We will kiss our costars.

"Yes, we have to kiss other women and many of them will be pretty damn hot, but it doesn't mean we want to date them. These people become more like family than lovers, even when it involves making out on-set—although that sounds grosser than it is. Remember, people are filming us and critiquing us, they are telling us where to put our hands and how to lean in for that kiss . . . and all the while they are up in our face with cameras. It's not sexy!"—Mark

She Says . . .

Don't give in to his every desire.

"Actors like to have what they want five minutes before they want it. They don't understand the concept of planning ahead or having to wait for anything. If he calls you, he wants to see you that night or even that minute, and he truly thinks that's okay. Sadly, too many of us let him believe that it is okay. After all, we know that if we don't come to meet him, he will call the next woman on his speed dial. Try not to give in to this. You are just enabling him to continue to act like a pompous ass. Instead, make him work for you. He will respect you for it."—Joanna

Ask yourself why you like him.

"If you like him only because he's an actor, then you're in the relationship for the wrong reasons. Take him off that pedestal. My friend was dating this actor turned Calvin Klein model and I knew that she was only into him because he was hot. He was on this huge billboard in Times Square in his underwear, and she used to walk by it on the street just so she could get the thrill of knowing that he was in her bed the night before. She didn't even like him; she just liked knowing that he was with her. I almost felt bad for him."—Carey

The Breakdown

Here's a look at the actor:

biggest turn on	He's passionate about what he does
biggest challenge	Getting him to commit
best way to get in touch	His cell phone
greatest perk	He's great in bed
best timing	When he's happy with his career

Talking Shop

Here's a list of key words and phrases that will help you speak his language:

Call sheet: A call sheet is a printed schedule of the day's work that is to be filmed and the people, places, and things needed. If he says he's at work all day and you don't trust him, check his call sheet.

Call time: The actual time he needs to be on the set.

Callback: Any follow-up interview or audition. Every actor is dying to get a callback!

Credits: A performer's experience, listed on his resume. Find out what his credits are. If he's in a movie or on a TV show, his credit should appear at the end. This is a big deal even if he's listed as "boy holding mop in soda shop." Let him know you are proud.

Extra: A performer hired as window dressing, commonly referred to as *background*. Your guy very well might be an extra in something, and the odd part is that his role might take days to shoot. Try not to make fun of this.

Head shot: A still photograph of your boyfriend taken by a professional photographer. If you've ever been to one of those dry cleaners in New York City or one of the famous delis where all the celebrities go, look up on the wall and you'll see a bunch of signed head shots. Make sure your guy has a stack of these and make him sign one for you. It may sound corny, but if the relationship fails, it's a great souvenir.

Open casting call: A casting call that is open to the public. There's a lot of waiting time and most often he won't get the outcome he's hoping for. Think *American Idol.*

Read-through: Usually the first rehearsal where the actors get together and read through the script. This gives the writers a chance to see where the writing needs to be tweaked. Your guy will be unreachable during a read-through, so don't expect him to leave his cell phone on or to check his messages.

Residuals: The fee paid to a performer for rebroadcast of a commercial, film, or television program. He can make a killing off residuals alone.

SAG: No, this has nothing to do with what happens to your body parts when you get older! SAG stands for the Screen Actors Guild, and your boyfriend should be a SAG member if he wants to work in Hollywood. Many agents won't consider representing actors unless they have a SAG card.

chapter 8 The Musician

"I dated a musician for six months. He had no money. He couldn't even afford to eat dinners out, but he had a record deal with a major record label. He'd sleep late, play a gig, write songs, sleep . . . I would go to his shows, listen to him practice, and I even went on tour with them for a few weeks. He always smelled of cigarettes, but there was something so sexy about him. Artsy guys can pull off a lot of things that regular guys can't. They make you believe that their issues are an acceptable part of the creative process."—Lauren

This guy is passionate and sexy. When he enters onto the stage he begins with a song about the woman who broke his heart, and when the women go wild he scans the crowd and then settles his gaze on you. Your knees weaken, literally, and you feel like the only woman in the room. Though your initial intent was to leave after one beer, now you are set on spending the entire evening in the front row. You hang on his every word, laughing at his little anecdotes in between sets, watching his hair fall in front of his face. This guy is everything you've been missing. He's raw, emotional, and incredibly sexy. And watching him pour his heart out onstage only reaffirms why you shouldn't be dating any more of those investment banker types. When his gig is over, he wipes the sweat from his forehead and throws his T-shirt into the crowd. You don't catch it, but you don't try either. Instead you buy a CD and you ask him to sign it. And instead of signing his name, he writes down his number. Sure, he's supposed to get your number, but just this once you let him dictate the rules. "Listen to song number eight," he says before you walk out the door. And when you go home you run to your CD player to hear the love song he wrote to "that woman in the crowd." Sounds like fate, right? Though it could be real (he might be a rock star and you might be the next Kate Hudson or Gwyneth Paltrow), chances are your night was more of a one-hit wonder. After all, part of his job is to make his fans love him.

His Look

Though he wants you to believe that all he cares about is the music, most likely he's put quite a bit of thought into his image, even down to whether he's going to wear the smelly green T-shirt to his gig or the smelly white one. Though each musician has his own image, depending upon the type of music he plays (rock, alternative, country, etc.), most musicians like to stay away from mainstream trends. Chances are he buys his clothes from vintage stores and places off the beaten path. These guys like to look original, but they like to be comfortable as well—lots of T-shirts, funky pants, worn-out jeans, vintage sport coats, and Converse sneakers.

His Vibe

Creative, passionate, sensitive, and romantic. Though this guy is very relaxed in many ways (he tends to be a bit flaky and absent-minded), he's also incredibly intense about his music. Musicians are true artists. Even after landing a record deal, it will still take years before he'll make any good money (unless he's the next *American Idol* winner). But, for the most part, musicians aren't driven by the financial aspect. In fact, many of them thrive on the instability and excitement of the unknown. And it's actually predictability that scares them more than anything. No musician wants things to get too rigid or safe. So what does this mean for you? Get used to a lack of funds, which means more creative, intimate, and oftentimes romantic dates. Get ready for picnics in the park, long walks on the beach, and endless trips to the music store to listen to CDs. Though this might sound romantic at first, it could wear on you.

His Hours

Full-time musicians work extremely late nights and don't see the light of day until the early afternoon. These guys dread the daylight and most of them don't get up much before 1 P.M., so don't expect him to join you for coffee in the morning. Chances are he's never even seen the *Today* show. Afternoons are spent writing new songs, rehearsing with the band, recording, or traveling from one city to the next. Gigs start as late as 11 P.M., followed by parties that last until 2 or 3 A.M. Don't be surprised if your guy calls you at 1 A.M. from some loud and crazy bar. Though this may seem inappropriate to you, this is actually not a booty call. In musician time, 1 A.M. is the equivalent of 8 P.M. our time. His most stressful times? When he's recording an album, releasing an album, promoting an album, or arguing with his band members. Note: Never call a full-time musician before 1 P.M.

Risk Factor

Female fans that constantly hit on him, odd hours, late nights, late mornings, constant rehearsals, mood swings, some sort of substance abuse, detailed songs about sex with his ex-girlfriends, parties, big egos, and lots of time on the road and away from you. If he's famous, make sure he struggled a bit before he found success. Those who experience instant success will expect everything to be handed to them.

Perks

Being serenaded privately, especially in bed. Being serenaded publicly, when all the women in the room are in love with your rock star boyfriend and he is singing to you. This guy is also more attentive and caring in bed than most any businessman. He's also very romantic and expressive. And, you never know, he could make tons of money down the line.

Has He Been Signed?

Here's a look at the music industry's five biggest record labels and some of the bands they represent:

- **Universal Music Group:** U2, Beck, No Doubt
- **Sony Music Group:** Michael Jackson, Lauryn Hill, Macy Gray
- **EMI Group:** Pink Floyd, Janet Jackson, Beastie Boys
- **Warner Brothers Music Group:** Phish, Kid Rock, Led Zeppelin
- **BMG Entertainment:** Dave Matthews, Outkast, Christina Aguilera

Will You Rule Him Out?

Before you decide, here's a look at what to expect when you are dating a musician.

Rule #1:
Music is his number one love.

A musician never clocks out. Instead, he spends his "off hours" thinking of new ways to improve his music, whether that means jotting down song lyrics in the middle of what you thought was a serious, intimate discussion, or thinking about new ways to entertain the audience while he's onstage. Make sure that you genuinely like his music, because otherwise your relationship will never work. Remember, this guy is putting his heart and soul into his music every day, hoping to be discovered. He will need your support and he will ask you for your advice. According to Laurie, "You need to be honest with him, but at the same time be sensitive to his work. He won't like it if you say everything is amazing, nor will he like it if you say 'that lyric sucks.' You have to find a balance. Be able to show your interest and support without being overly critical. These guys are supersensitive."

Rule #2:
Get to know his band members, and you will get to know the real him.

If you don't get along with his band members, it's going to cause conflict. These guys pretty much come with the territory. He will travel with them, practice with them, and even take on some of their good and bad habits. So unless you want to be the next Yoko Ono, start making nice. Besides, you can find out a lot about your guy by hanging out with his band. For starters, how do these guys spend their time? And what do they do to relax after they've played a gig? Do they go home and play Sony PlayStation like a bunch of high school kids, or are they trashing hotel rooms, partying with fans, and sleeping with groupies? Whatever your guy's band is doing, chances are he's doing the same thing.

Rule #3:
Women will hit on him and he will let them.

Musicians have an image to uphold, regardless of whether or not it's the truth. There are plenty of famous musicians who are in relationships, maybe even married, but they don't let the public know because it may change the way their fans feel about them. Musicians are passionate and sensitive, but they are also a bit mysterious and that draws us in. So don't take it personally if he doesn't shout out that he's taken to everyone in the world. Still, that doesn't mean it doesn't suck when he points to a cute woman in the crowd and brings her onstage. Just make sure he doesn't start making out with her, because that's just not cool.

Rule #4:
His lifestyle will be completely different from yours.

He has odd hours, random sleep habits, and his own way of getting things done (and it may take three times as long as you would imagine it to take). Full-time musicians sleep until 1 P.M. and go to bed around 3 A.M. When your day ends (assuming you work a stable nine-to-five job), his is just beginning. Expect to hear from him at odd hours from random venues. Half the time he'll call you from a gig where you'll hear loud noises and people screaming around him. This doesn't mean he's having a blast without you. It just means that he's in a loud bar. Stacy says, "Whatever you do, don't start a fight with him while he's on the road. There's nothing worse than fighting with your boyfriend long-distance, knowing that there are female fans everywhere around him and that he's pissed at you. Plus, even if you make up, you'll feel unsettled until you get to see one other."

Rule #5:
He will sing songs about being in love with his ex-girlfriends.

This is inevitable and there's nothing you can do about it. Whatever you do, don't read into all his lyrics and try to decipher what's going on in his head—just don't do it. It will drive you crazy and the reality is that he probably doesn't even remember what he was thinking at the time that he wrote that song. Musicians like to sing about everything. They will recall the smell of their ex-girlfriend's hair, the color of her eyes, the texture of her skin. . . . And it's bound to make you sick. Whatever you do, don't question him about it, because he will interpret your curiosity as jealousy (which it is) and the last thing he wants is to feel that you are controlling his music. If it makes you feel any better, chances are he's written a few songs about you as well. Just hope that he records them when the two of you are still together; otherwise, he might butcher them. Lauren says, "My boyfriend used to write these romantic songs about me and he'd serenade me privately, referring to me as 'the beautiful girl.' A few months after we broke up, he released a new CD. It turned out that my songs were in there, but they were changed. I went from being the beautiful girl to being the girl he buried in the backyard!"

Rule #6:
You will fall for him quickly.

Musicians are passionate and romantic; they are open and very easy to fall for. Unfortunately, it's hard to know if they have really fallen for you. Unlike lawyers or doctors, musicians share their innermost thoughts with you right away, so chances are you'll feel more connected to this guy after one night than you did with your ex-boyfriend after one year. Just remember that being expressive and emotional is in his nature, and just because he tells you how beautiful you are doesn't mean that he wants to marry you. This guy is much more spiritual and passionate than your typical guy. Musicians are in love with the idea of falling in love. They thrive on experiencing life and they yearn for the kind of intensity that love brings. This doesn't mean he's using you; it just means that you need to check in with yourself before you put your heart on the line.

Rule #7:
He's not as afraid of commitment as he is of monotony.

Many musicians actually want relationships. What they don't want is to feel complacent, bored, or mediocre. If things get too stable in their romantic lives, many will duck out of the relationship. Artists need to experience life, and they believe that they need to experience a certain level of pain in order to feel truly alive.

He Says . . .

Yes, we lose track of time.

"When I am in the middle of writing a song, I will completely lose myself in my work, and that can cause major problems with my girlfriend. I have a tendency to shut off my phone and lock myself in the studio for hours without any idea of what time it is. Oddly, this is how some of us get our best work done, so please don't get pissed at us for it."—Darin

Lots of us actually want a girlfriend.

"Many of us are very happy to have someone stable and supportive around that loves us for who we really are and not because we are musicians. Even though it's flattering to get hit on by female fans, we know by now that it has very little to do with us and a lot to do with the fact that we are musicians. As exhilarating as it is to be on tour, it can also be pretty lonely at times. We are in unfamiliar cities, sleeping in hotels, and lots of us crave that constant, that person to call at the end of the night, the one who is waiting for us to come home."—Ari

Just because we're musicians doesn't mean we're party-boy womanizers.

"Just because we can get out there and perform in front of tons of people doesn't mean that we have the guts to ask out any woman offstage. My band members laugh at me, but I am actually a pretty shy guy in person and that's part of the reason why I love music, because it allows me to express myself in ways that I could never do in the real world. So before you go making any assumptions, take a look at who we might be and not just what we do.—Brian

If a guy likes you, he should call you, regardless of how busy he is.

"Yes, his hours are completely different than yours, especially when he's on the road. But if he really likes you, he should be able to call. Don't get pissed at him if he calls late at night from a loud venue with screaming fans in the background. It's not easy for us to find the time or the privacy to call, so give us credit where credit is due. Beware of the guy that calls you only when he's in your city. That's the biggest sign that he's playing you."—Josh

She Says . . .

Give him space when he needs it.

"Understand that even though they are very tight with their band members, they also have moments where they don't see eye to eye and that can be incredibly frustrating. My boyfriend needs his space most when this happens. He usually gets so frustrated and the last thing he wants to do is talk to me about all the details of who wants what. This is when he shuts down and I have come to learn that he might need to do that. I also respect the space he needs when he's rehearsing or recording. I am also an artist, so I know how easy it is for someone to disrupt the creative flow, especially during recording. Even though he keeps his phone on vibrate, just that can trip up his rhythm and possibly ruin a great idea he was following."—Alison

Have your friends and family meet him outside of the context of his band.

"If you really love this guy, it should be because of who he is and not what he does. My husband is a musician and when I knew that I was in love with him, I made sure my parents met him when he wasn't performing or practicing or hanging out with the band. People in your life should get to know your guy the way that you know him. They should know him as a person first and then as a musician. Now they make him sing for them every time we have a family event, but that's okay. It was just important to me that they knew him first before they knew his music."—**Jennifer**

Try not to get too jealous when women drape all over him.

"He will have women flirting with him, even if they are women that are in the business. Still, don't get too jealous when you see a woman flirting with him, especially if you have no idea who that woman is. One time I got pissed off watching this woman flirt with my boyfriend, and so I came up behind him and pulled him away from her to give him a big kiss. It turns out she was a magazine editor doing a story on emerging artists! Though I'm sure she was flirting with him, I still felt like an idiot. The truth is that musicians need to be liked and they need people to be interested and excited about their work, even if those people are hot, single women."—**Jenna**

Ask yourself if you can handle the uncertainty.

"Although the lifestyle of an artist can be extremely exciting and wonderful, it can also be very frightening. And those who haven't reached a level of financial success by a certain point feel their time ticking away. Both my boyfriend and I are struggling musicians and even though we chose not to take a safer route, there is something to be said for kind of knowing what your life is going to look like. The hardest part is that there's no way to really help it." —Alison

The Breakdown

The musician:

biggest turn on	He's passionate about what he does
biggest challenge	Financial stability
best way to get in touch	After 1 P.M. on his cell phone
greatest perk	Being privately serenaded
best timing	When he's home

Talking Shop

Here's a list of key words and phrases that will help you speak his language:

Band manager: He represents your guy on everything to do with his music career. Get to know this guy because chances are he'll rarely leave your boyfriend's side. Note: It is not unheard of for girlfriends and managers to butt heads. Both have strong opinions on what is best for the band.

Book: A band is "booked" at a club if the group is scheduled to play there. Your guy will be superexcited when his band gets booked at various hot spots.

Demo: A "demonstration" recording that is meant to give a sample of an artist's music. Artists will create demos to get people excited and interested in their music.

Gig: A live performance at which multiple artists perform, usually for free, to gain exposure among people who work in the music industry, and sometimes the public. Guys with "gigs" lined up are usually struggling musicians and not famous rock stars.

Gold: If a record goes gold it means the record sells over 500,000 copies.

Headliner: Hopefully your boyfriend is the headliner for the night. A headliner is the artist who plays last at a concert. It's the more well-known act that the majority of the audience goes to see.

Opener: An artist that is considered to be less well known, who performs before the better-known artist. Don't fret if your boyfriend is the opener. Britney Spears was once the opener for *NSYNC, and now look at her.

Platinum: No, he's not talking about your wedding band, so don't even let your mind go there. Instead he's talking about his record "going platinum." Although if his record goes platinum, he can afford to buy you diamonds. When a record goes platinum it means it sells over 1 million copies.

Set: The songs that an artist performs at a particular concert. Don't leave before your guy has played his entire set. It's like leaving your best friend's wedding before the cake.

Shelved: This is not a good thing. When a recording is shelved, it means that a record company decided not to release it to the public. This can be devastating to an artist who worked hard to get his album released. Be extra kind to him if this happens.

Single: No, this has nothing to do with his marital status. A single is a song that an artist or record label decides to release to the public separately from other songs. Radio stations, press, MTV, and the artists themselves are supposed to focus on this song, as it's expected to be the most popular. An album can have many singles, although they are released one at a time.

Sound check: A rehearsal before the actual performance that ensures the sound levels are appropriate at the concert venue. Most musicians show up early to a show in order to do a sound check.

chapter 9 The Writer

He's curious, passionate, and creative. Writers are very clever individuals, so expect to be creatively courted. Yes, finally you'll be swept off your feet by someone who's charming, articulate, well read, and intuitive! Writers leave the best voice mail messages (they're not afraid to sing into your machine or act goofy), they actually write in their cards to you instead of just signing their name (or first initial) at the bottom, and their e-mails will leave you laughing yourself silly at your desk chair. And get this: they're great communicators, at least when they are feeling good about themselves. But before you coin them the best of the bunch, you should also know that writers are typically neurotic, emotional, and self-deprecating (which can be funny to a point). And they can't help but overanalyze their every move. Oh, and when they're not happy with their writing, they tend to be an absolute mess, unable to concentrate on anything. Much like musicians, writers put their craft on the line each and every day, hoping that others will appreciate (and validate) what they've created. And when this doesn't happen, no matter how confident or used to it they should be, they are crushed. So whether he's sulking over script notes from the studio or an editor's last-minute decision to pull his cover story from the magazine, chances are your writer guy will go into hiding because he's feeling intellectually vulnerable. The good news? His desire for space has nothing to do with another woman. Most likely he's locked himself in some secret office with his laptop and a small window.

His Look

Though he cares about his looks, this guy's not overly caught up in material possessions. A writer who's too preoccupied with his exterior image or too caught up in what's "in fashion" will not be taken seriously among his peers. Instead, he's supposed to appear as more of a starving artist, or at least a slightly tortured one. Plus, in reality he's much more concerned with his work (is it sharp, fresh, funny, tight?) than he is with the latest fashion in men's jeans.

His Vibe

Confident and comfortable one minute, neurotic, insecure, and socially awkward the next. Writers experience everything in poignant detail, which is a good thing on the one hand (they will be sensitive to your feelings) and a bad thing on the other hand (they are hyperaware of their own issues and sensitivities). Expect to have lots of conversations about other people, their personalities, their actions, their issues, etc. Though it may seem like intellectual gossip, he's actually trying to flesh out the main characters in his new screenplay or novella.

His Hours

It depends on the kind of writing he's doing, and what stage he's in. Journalists are at the beck and call of the stories they are chasing. Some stories take as few as two days to cover, while others could take as long as two months. Screenwriters and novelists have the most freedom and flexibility. They are given a deadline and told to go off and write. TV writers have more of a set nine-to-five schedule, unless they're writing a specific episode, in which case they are sent off (albeit for a much shorter time) to get the script done. As for advertising copywriters, they have a more traditional work schedule with crazy hours and late nights accumulating before client pitch meetings. Though there are many different types of writers, one thing's for sure: This guy will never stop thinking, observing, reading, and, of course, writing. Don't be surprised if your guy disappears for huge chunks of time to purge his thoughts, only to reappear completely invigorated or, in the worst case, frustrated.

Risk Factor

It's an isolating industry with a lot of rejection. Though some writers may make tons of money, the majority of writers out there barely get by. It's an excruciatingly competitive field with no guarantees. Many writers also feel as though they need to experience things first before they can accurately write about them (regardless of what they may be). Don't be surprised if your guy starts experimenting in bizarre ways. Unless you are bothered by this behavior, chalk it up to research.

Perks

He's creative, passionate, and witty. Most likely, he loves what he does for a living, even though it drives him crazy at times. If he is a screenwriter and he makes it big, he can make tons of money, selling scripts for hundreds of thousands of dollars in one shot. TV writers also make a phenomenal living, plus they have the structure of a nine-to-five job (complete with an office!), and a two-month vacation when taping stops (yes, this means more vacation time with you). Freelance writers make their own hours and they get great freebies; for example, celebrity journalists go to red carpet events, music award shows, and opening nights on Broadway (you might get to be his plus-one), whereas food critics get to wine and dine in the top restaurants for free.

Will You Rule Him Out?

Before you decide, here's a look at what to expect when you are dating a writer.

Rule #1:
Don't even think of discussing the status of your relationship when he's on deadline.

Writers tend to block out everyone when they are on deadline. They forget to pee, shower, pay their bills, answer the phone, take out the trash, you name it. So, even though you're being neglected (chances are he hasn't even returned your calls), it's best to discuss your feelings once he's handed in his work. The reality is that he's probably too panicked and obsessed with his work to even address your concerns properly. Don't take this personally. Writers have the ability to procrastinate until they reach a point where they are completely screwed. If he does this, chances are his best work occurs when he's driven by fear.

Rule #2:
He's surprisingly indecisive and in desperate need of your approval.

Don't be surprised if you find him reading lines to you over and over again, wondering which one you prefer. As confident as he is, he's also so caught up in his work and isolated from everyone else that he's dying for a fresh perspective or maybe just approval. "I went out with this screenwriter for a while and we used to go to his place and he'd make me read his script with him in the room," says Sherri. "He'd stand there looking over my shoulder and waiting for me to laugh at certain places and cry at others. It was so much pressure, and then at the end he'd want me to tell him what I thought. Truthfully, I was nervous that I would say the wrong thing and make him not like me."

Rule #3:
He will have a hard time separating his fictional characters from his real life.

Make sure you set boundaries. "Sometimes I felt like he was more serious with his main female character than he was with me. Seriously, I started to get jealous," says Kerri. "You have to set some boundaries with a writer because otherwise he'll spend his time talking with you about made-up people instead of asking you how your day was. One day I was telling him about a friend of mine who lost her mother. And as I was talking, I realized that he was drifting off a bit, thinking about something. Then he sort of refocused and he said something like, 'That's it! Maybe I'll have her lose her mother at the end.' Of course, he was talking about his main character! I was so furious that he was that selfish."

Rule #4:
He will appear lost and vulnerable in between projects.

Writers are incredibly passionate people who spend every hour of every day thinking about their story lines and running different scenarios through their head. Though they tend to appear stressed and neurotic just before a deadline, they also appear lost and deflated a few days after a deadline. Handing in a script or a completed manuscript is an incredible accomplishment, but once the achievement wears off, a writer is left with a blank slate. Finding that next project can often be confusing.

Rule #5:
He's petrified of mediocrity.

Writers, not unlike musicians, feel that they have to experience a certain amount of pain in order to write well, and sometimes they'll even sabotage something good out of fear of complacency. "I went out with a guy for over a year and then one day he just freaked out and told me that he was losing his edge. He said things were getting too comfortable and settled for him, and that in order to make it as a writer he needed to be raw and exposed. I knew that he didn't want to end our relationship, but he did it anyway. And it was like he was trying to create pain for himself so that he had something to write about," says Jennifer.

Rule #6:
He will see his own life experiences, no matter how tragic or bizarre, as future writing material.

These guys are definitely willing to take risks and experience everything, so just make sure that you're not part of some writing assignment. Writers tend to experience things for research purposes, or at least they like to use that excuse when they get caught doing something that they shouldn't be doing. "One guy I was dating was making a film about the drug scene and he was so obsessed with experiencing the mindset of his characters that he ended up asking me on a date and having me over for dinner and pot brownies. Once I realized what had happened I was too high to care," says Sherri.

Rule #7:

He will share your most intimate secrets with the rest of his workshop or writers' room.

Yes, he will bring up everything from how you look when you wake up in the morning to what you sound like when you are having an orgasm. One thing every novelist learns is to "write what you know," so while whatever he shares with his writing workshop may be "fiction," chances are he's pilfering true stories from his (or your) life experience. The same is true for the television writer, who gets together with colleagues in the writers' room to brainstorm realistic scenarios for their characters. It's only inevitable that your guy will bring up something that you two did or a funny thing that you told him in confidence. Chances are everyone else in the room is doing the same thing, so while it might be embarrassing, try not to take it personally. It's actually kind of funny when you think that something that happened to you might happen to someone on *The OC* or *Scrubs,* or be the emotional center of your man's latest book.

He Says . . .

Expect us to tune you out when we're writing.

"We can disappear for hours on end, but that's just the way most writers work. If I could tell any woman what to expect, I would say expect him to disappear for days. Writers need their space, especially when they are on deadline. If you can't give it to him, the relationship will never work."—Carl

Not all writers have the same schedule.

"Unlike screenwriters and novelists, our job is not done the minute we hand over our script or manuscript. I had a girlfriend who used to date a screenwriter, so she just assumed that once I handed in my episode, my work was done. In TV you spend hours on the set with the cast and crew, making sure that they are delivering your lines the way you intended, and most of that time you are completely unreachable. It's not like you can let your cell phone ring in the middle of a scene."—Josh

She Says . . .

He has this amazing, flexible schedule.

"Many of these guys make their own schedules, and although that might mean he'll choose to spend late nights and weekends at his computer, it also means that he can be flexible with his time and carve out a little for the two of you. Even if he's superswamped, at least he'll know when things are easing up, which is far better than being at the beck and call of a boss."—Karen

What Kind of Writer Is He?

- **Screenwriter:** He thinks in scenes. This guy loves the movies. He's completely tapped into the Hollywood scene and knows of every well-known director, screenwriter, agent, and actor in the business. If he's an aspiring screenwriter, chances are he spends his days obsessing over films, taking writing classes, and working on his "top secret" screenplay. If he's a working screenwriter, he's most likely a bit more realistic. He writes not only what he loves but also what he knows will sell.
- **Advertising copy writer:** He thinks in quick, catchy sentences and he pays attention to things like brand image and logo size. This guy works on a regular nine-to-five schedule (more like 10 to 6 P.M.) and he's usually laid-back and content, though deep down he wishes he was out there being more creative. Expect him to work closely with his partner (every copywriter has an art director partner), who just might be a woman.
- **Ghostwriter:** No one wants to admit he is a ghostwriter, and yet he will probably try to make you think that this is what he really wants. A ghostwriter is hired to write someone else's book. Though he will be paid, he will not receive any recognition. It's a thankless job.
- **Magazine freelance writer:** When he's not pitching new article ideas he can be found surfing the Internet for research, conducting phone interviews, attending shows, openings, conventions (depending on what story he's covering), or ferociously writing on his computer to meet deadlines.

The Breakdown

Here's what you need to know about the writer:

biggest turn on	He's passionate about what he does
biggest challenge	Making a living
best way to get in touch	E-mail (he's always on his computer, unless he's shooting)
greatest perk	Hiatus
best timing	Two days after he's made his deadline

Talking Shop

Here's a list of key words and phrases that will help you speak his language:

Agent: By this point you should know all about this guy (see Chapter 4). Most working writers have agents who represent them and help them sell their work. This guy will constantly be on the phone with his agent.

Deadline: AKA your own personal hell. Writers freak out during their deadline, which means most likely he'll be moody, aloof, and stressed. A deadline is the date given to a writer by his editor or producer to indicate when he should be finished with his story, screenplay, episode, novel, etc.

Edit: To review a piece of writing, marking and correcting grammatical, spelling, and factual errors. The editing process also often includes the shortening or lengthening of articles to fit available space, rewriting headlines and subheads, tweaking jokes, story lines, character descriptions, etc. Be careful around your boyfriend when his work comes back heavily edited. He will feel deflated and vulnerable.

Manager: Kind of like an agent but less smooth and typically more genuine. Many screenwriters have managers and agents. Managers can do everything an agent can do and more. They have the clout to get films made due to their contacts and unique position in the industry. And they are often more attentive to the individual needs of their writers, which is why some writers are closer friends with their managers than they are with their agents. Note: Get to know this guy. He's just another person your boyfriend will turn to in a time of need.

Notes: Refers to the comments/edits given to a script by a development executive, agent, manager, or writing partner. No matter how confident your guy is, he will most likely be disheartened if he receives a lot of notes on any given piece of work. Give him a little encouragement and space when this happens. Writers are emotional creatures, but they eventually bounce back.

Outline: A writer's guide, either for his own use or for the use of his advisors (i.e., editors, producers). Nonfiction authors will have to include an outline in their book proposal in order to sell the concept, whereas TV writers have to submit an outline before writing each episode. Though writing an outline may appear to be easy, it can actually be incredibly difficult and frustrating.

Pitch: Typically a verbal conversation, also called a *sell,* as the writer is briefly selling the idea by pitching its benefits to the buyer. The best writers are known to be excellent at pitching ideas.

Query letter: A one-page letter designed to entice the reader to ask for the script or book for further evaluation.

On spec: A magazine article, manuscript, TV, or film script that is written on speculation that it can be sold upon completion with no agreement or contract with a principal. New writers often write pieces on spec with the hopes of proving their writing ability.

Work for hire: Paid writing work usually without a byline. The writer does not own any of the writing or have any claims to it. This is not the ideal situation for a writer. Most writers want credit for their work.

part 3: The Handymen

He's that macho-looking guy who's hard at work replacing the engine in your car, rewiring your apartment, or laying the foundation for that new building across the street from your house. You watch him in awe, a quintessential manly man complete with grease stains, tool belt, hardhat, and protective goggles. He appears strong and capable.

And while he's not the most articulate or "cultural" of men—this guy's a bit rough around the edges—he's so incredibly handy that you almost don't care. After all, what's so great about dating a cultural connoisseur if he can't hook up your TV?

the lowdown

his job	personality traits	most commonly used gadget	how he spends his weekends	his biggest concern
construction worker	focused, project-oriented	his tools	fixing things	he doesn't have one
electrician	laid back, resourceful	his toolbox	working odd jobs	safety
automotive technician	focused, thorough, problem-solving	his car	upgrading his car	keeping up with the latest car technology

chapter 10 The Construction Worker

He's that big, strong-looking man strapped to the side of a building, surrounded by cement trucks, wooden planks, and other sweaty men in hardhats and tool belts. You know exactly where he'll be each day, including when he takes his cigarette breaks (these guys are on a very tight schedule), and so you time it perfectly, making sure to walk by him the moment he sits down for lunch. He whistles at you, of course, and even though the whole thing's completely contrived, you can't help but think that something about this guy, covered in dirt and sweat, and epitomizing the term "man's man" as he grins up at you, totally turns you on. You imagine what it would be like to take him home with you and let him have his way with your broken TV set and coffee table. And when he was finally done, the two of you would share cold beers on your porch before jumping into the shower to cool off. Sounds nice, right? But before you slot this guy as a fantasy-fulfilling, one-time fling, listen to this: construction guys make great boyfriends.

His Look

Tan, if he's working outside. As for his wardrobe, think hardhat, toolbelt, baggy jeans, and insulated workboots. Expect him to have a strong build regardless of whether he works out—after all, he spends his days lifting heavy machinery. Don't be surprised when you hold his hand and it feels like sandpaper. These guys have more cuts and calluses than an Olympic gymnast. And don't even think of suggesting a manicure.

His Vibe

Strong, assertive, and a possibly a bit rough around the edges. He's a quintessential guy's guy, which means he loves drinking beer, driving trucks, racing cars, and of course, talking about women. At work he may refer to girls as everything from chicks to bitches. Try not to take this personally; it's a construction thing, and not necessarily the way he feels about you.

His Hours

Obscenely early mornings. Most construction guys are at work as early as 6 A.M., which means he'll be up by 5 A.M. every day. Days end around 2 P.M., but those who want to move ahead and make more money often work overtime or take odd jobs like snow plowing in the wintertime (which could involve a 2 A.M. wakeup call to plow the streets before rush hour). Weekends might include a few hours on Saturday, but again, that's only if he chooses to work weekends.

Risk Factor

Expect him to come home from work feeling physically exhausted, which means if you want to see him, chances are you'll be ordering in dinner and watching him pass out in front of the TV. As for his salary, he can make as little as $18,000 or as much as $80,000 if he works overtime and takes on odd freelance jobs. And if he opens his own company, anything's possible!

Perks

He's incredibly handy, which means he'll fix your broken TV, build you a shelf, coffee table, wall unit, you name it. These guys are also surprisingly anal—yes, they make their beds, clean their apartments, and even pay their bills on time. Plus, have you ever seen a guy wear a hardhat and tool belt while operating heavy machinery? It's pretty damn sexy.

Will You Rule Him Out?

Before you decide, here's a look at what to expect when you are dating a guy in construction.

Rule #1:

He *will* act different when he's at work.

Though you should be able to get in touch with him during the day, providing that his cell phone works at the site and he chooses to answer it, don't expect him to expose his sensitive side while on the job. In fact, you'll be lucky if he gives you two minutes of his undivided attention. "I try not to call my boyfriend at work too much because he's never alone when I call him and he's usually in the middle of something that could be pretty dangerous. He might be operating a crane, driving a tractor, or hanging from the side of a building, and the idea of him not paying attention to what he's doing really freaks me out. Plus, he acts completely different when he's around the other guys. The construction site is like a tank of testosterone, and these guys turn into macho tough guys when they are together. There are times when I honestly can't help but laugh, because when he's with those guys, my boyfriend sounds like a complete jackass. Whatever you do, don't take this personally, just laugh."—Ally

Rule #2:

He will come home physically exhausted.

It's not like he's been sitting at his desk making phone calls all day, girls. Construction guys are up as early as 5 A.M. each morning and they spend their days lifting and operating heavy machinery in all kinds of weather. When they get home, most of them are physically exhausted and many of them just want to shower, have a few beers, smoke a few cigarettes, order in food, and lay on the couch. This will make for many cozy nights together, but it could also get annoying if you're in the mood to go out and socialize. "You definitely have to readjust your schedule and your lifestyle if you're dating a construction guy. My last boyfriend was an accountant and we used to go out to nice dinners all the time. These guys are more low-maintenance. They'd rather order in and unless someone is coming over to their house, they're usually not up for making weekday plans. Just remember this has nothing to do with how he feels about you, and everything to do with the physically exhausting day he just had. I've completely changed my schedule. Now I am in bed with him by 10 P.M on weekdays." —Mary

Rule #3:
He's surprisingly anal.

Yes, these guys make their beds, wash their dishes, and pay their bills on time! In fact, your guy might even be more organized than you are. "My boyfriend can't stand when something is out of place. His place is extremely neat and he's always on top of everything, from the car insurance and inspection to the phone bill. He even gets annoyed with me when he sees that I haven't fixed something in my apartment, and usually it's something that I don't even notice was broken, like a hinge coming off a door. I think it's because construction is such a precise industry and everything has to be measured and accounted for. Plus, these guys have incredibly structured days. Even their coffee breaks are planned and timed." —Stacey

Rule #4:
When he's not working paid jobs, he's busy working "friendly jobs."

The good news is that these guys are some of the most generous boyfriends you'll ever meet. They'll help you move into your new place without you even asking. They'll build you a wall unit, install crown molding, create a walk-in closet, you name it. And while this might be a huge plus for you, it can be a huge pain when he's doing it for every friend he's ever made since high school. "Everyone is always asking him to fix something for them, and it's not even like he minds. He loves it. I used to get so annoyed because between his early mornings, overtime, and freelance jobs we barely got to spend time together. And then when we finally had the opportunity he would tell me that he and the guys were going to help a friend with a move. But now I realize that he is going to find a construction project regardless of whether someone needs his help. He and his friends are always building something or updating something in their house and that's just because it's what they love to do."—Kim

Rule #5:
Chances are, he's not thinking about you during the day.

No, this guy is not surfing the Internet all day, staring at your screen name on Instant Message, and wondering whether or not he should say "what's up." Instead he's hanging from a building, removing scaffolding with twenty other guys in

90-degree heat. Though he may break for ten minutes every two hours to have a smoke, drink a soda, and whistle at a few hot women, most likely he won't use any of that time to call you. Why? First of all, regardless of what his real personality is like, when he's around these guys, he's playing the role of tough badass guy, not sensitive, let-me-hold-the-door-open-for-you guy. Second, he's in construction work mode, which means he's concentrating on whether or not the wall he just built will support the house he's working on, not whether he should surprise you with roses or chocolates. And, levelheaded, confident woman that you are, you realize that this is exactly where his head should be while on the job. So before you panic and wonder what he's thinking regarding the status of your relationship, remember this: you most likely won't enter his thoughts until much later in the day.

Rule #6:

He's not as predictable as you might think.

True, this guy has no filter. He will curse a lot, say anything that comes to his mind, no matter how it sounds, and may speak more crudely than you'd like him to about women. But here's the interesting part: he will also open the car door for you, pay for your meals, buy you nice gifts, and fix anything in your house that needs fixing. And most of these guys would rather have a serious long-term girlfriend than a series of one-night stands. "My brother is a construction worker and so are a lot of the guys I hang out with," says Alyssa. "And they are all pretty similar. They love trucks, they all smoke and drink beer, and they are all tough and macho. But when you spend time alone with them, they can be very sweet. So try to be patient with them, and give them a chance. They are totally different when they are one-on-one, and sometimes they just need a little coaxing."

He Says . . .

It's hard for us to give up control, especially when it comes to fixing things around the house.

"When I know how to get something done fast and cheap, the last thing I want to do is hire someone else to do the job, especially in my own house. This usually creates problems with my girlfriend because she can't understand why I won't spend that free time with her instead. If I could offer any advice, it would be to try to understand that this is what we do for a living, and if we can apply it to our own homes, we want to be able to do that. It has nothing to do with whether or not we want to spend time with you. And it doesn't mean we are avoiding you, either. For the most part, construction guys are pretty assertive people. If the guy you are with isn't happy, he'll most likely tell it to you straight."—Frank

We need a girl that's low-maintenance.

"The last thing I want is to come home from a long day of work and feel like I have to entertain my girlfriend. Sometimes it's great having someone to come home to and lay on the couch with, but other times I feel like I can't handle all the obligations. I think we need a certain kind of girl; a girl that gets what we do and can understand why we do it."—Steve

She Says . . .

Don't be so quick to judge this guy.

"Although he won't make as much money as a banker, these guys have a huge amount of talent and self-worth. Their jobs take a lot of skill and precision and some of them go on to become landscapers or set designers, so be careful not to underestimate the work they do, or their potential for success. Plus, they take pride in what they do and they are generally very diligent and responsible. I went out with a crane operator for two years and he had every good quality that I look for in a man."—Alyson

They are crappy communicators.

"These guys are not great with the phone, so don't be surprised if you leave him a message and he never calls back. Though he always carries his cell phone on the job, chances are he won't pick it up, especially if he doesn't recognize the number. Oh, and don't be surprised if his outgoing message is something like, 'yo,' and then you hear the beep. These guys don't need to be concerned about sounding 'professional.' Don't get discouraged if your guy seems impossible to get in touch with. Half these guys walk around with their mailboxes full and they never empty them. I used to have to text my boyfriend ten times before I could get him to call back!"—Alyssa

The Breakdown

Here's what you need to know about the construction worker:

biggest turn on	Seeing him in action
biggest challenge	Getting him to stop fixing things
best way to get in touch	His work cell phone
greatest perk	He can fix anything
best timing	Weekends

Building Blocks

Just because he's drilling holes on your sidewalk doesn't mean that's what he'll be doing for the rest of your life. Here's a look at his career options.

- **Landscaper:** The more artistic, design-oriented guys tend to move away from construction and toward landscaping. Just think, he could have flexible hours and his very own business. Plus landscapers work with no more than four or five guys at a time, which means no more talking about girls 24/7.
- **General contractor:** This guy works closely with the developer throughout the project. Unlike construction workers, the general contractor no longer plays a direct role in the actual construction. Instead these guys manage the entire process from selection and hiring to budget and timing.
- **Movie set designer:** Yep, your construction guy could find himself designing the set for the next Jennifer Aniston movie. Many of these guys know how to build sets quickly and for little money, which makes them perfect for Hollywood. The good news is that he will now have a "sexy job." The bad news is that there are plenty of beautiful women for him to gawk at.

Talking Shop

Here's a list of key words and phrases that will help you speak his language:

Apron: No, your guy is not turning metrosexual before your very eyes. The apron has nothing to do with cooking. Instead it refers to the piece below the sill of a window, installed to cover the rough edge of the wall finish.

Butt joint: Oh, the many ways to creatively misinterpret this term. A butt joint refers to the point where the ends of two timbers meet.

Cricket: No, he is not referring to the sport (if you can call it that), or the small, noisy bug. A cricket is actually a second roof that is built on top of the primary roof to increase its slope.

Keeper: While he might more frequently use this term in reference to the stunning, wonderful lady in his life (i.e., "she's a keeper"), a keeper is also a metal latch in a door frame.

King stud: No, for once he's not referring to himself. A king stud is actually the vertical frame of a window or door opening.

Mushroom: This is not a food or drug reference. A mushroom describes when the top of a concrete pier spreads out and hardens to become wider than the foundation wall thickness.

Party wall: No, he's not having a party without you. If he's busy building a "party wall," it simply means that he's building a wall that's common to adjoining buildings. In other words, both owners share the same wall on either side.

chapter 11 The Electrician

"I used to date the intellectual types; doctors, lawyers, finance guys. But dating an electrician has opened me up to a whole new world. I've found beautiful qualities in my boyfriend that I've never found in a man before. It feels simpler, more old-fashioned; the way dating is supposed to be. With the other guys everything was very 'what have you done for me lately'—they couldn't wait to move on to the next thing." —Lisa

He's that adorable-looking guy who just entered your living room, the one with the tool belt, toolbox, workboots, and that pair of perfectly distressed jeans. You introduce yourself, and then show him the layout of your apartment, pointing to the areas that need work. He focuses, immediately. And even though a part of you wishes he'd take more time to check you out, the other part of you is totally turned on by his desire to fix your things. Still, you duck into your bathroom to let your hair down (you had no idea this guy was going to be so hot) and then return to his side with a tall glass of water. And just as you set the glass beside his toolbox, it happens. He looks down at you from his ladder with those I-can-fix-anything-you-need eyes, and says, "This job might take a while." You know that means it will cost you more money, but you also know that it means he'll be there a lot . . .

His Look

He's far from metrosexual. This guy's a manly man, which means no dress shirts, slacks, or trips to the dry cleaners. In fact, chances are he doesn't own anything that will wrinkle. Still, he's got a lot of gear. Expect him to have everything from insulated workboots and water-resistant pants to goggles. Catch him on his way to work and you might confuse him for someone heading into combat.

His Vibe

Serious and focused while he's working, easygoing and playful when he's not. Most of these guys love what they do. Though some of them spend their days working alone, others spend their days surrounded by plumbers, painters, builders, etc. What does this mean for you? The more guys he works with, the rougher around the edges he will seem.

His Hours

It depends on the time of year and the type of electrician he is. While construction electricians (those who install electrical wiring) are often affected by seasons—they are much busier in the summer months—maintenance electricians (those who run maintenance checks on existing systems) are not. Still, maintenance electricians have the more unpredictable hours, which could include late nights, weekends, and an on-call schedule that could have them coming and going at all hours.

Risk Factor

You have no way of checking up on him or knowing where he is all day (he has no secretary, assistant, or office that he goes to) and some days he'll have no cell phone coverage. Plus, when he does come home, chances are he's physically exhausted. Remember, these guys spend their days working in tight spaces with no heat, air conditioning, or light. What does this mean for you? The last thing he wants to do when he gets home from work is to fix your problems, and yes, that includes your broken-down boiler.

Perks

He's old-fashioned and chivalrous. He'll carry your bags, drive you to the airport, and help you move furniture into your new place. Plus he's great at fixing things. He'll reroute your pipes, install your TV, rewire your living room, and fix your air conditioning.

Will You Rule Him Out?

Before you decide, here's a look at what to expect when you are dating an electrician.

Rule #1:

Don't ask him to fix your things in the beginning of the relationship.

Whatever you do, don't bombard him with your electrical problems right away. He may feel like you are using him. Plus, it's not like he's going to charge you, which means he's losing money by taking time away from paid jobs. "It's okay to ask him to help you with the little things," says Lisa. "These guys are great with the casual things, and they can get them done fast. My boyfriend checked out my car when it didn't sound good; he fixed my seatbelt when it was broken; he even rerouted my pipes when the vent in my kitchen smelled."

The relationship problems occur with the bigger things, and according to a number of girlfriends, you have to set boundaries early on. "Let them know that you need to get something fixed, and that if they can't do it, you completely understand, but if that's the case you need to hire someone to get the job done," says Lisa. "A lot of guys get territorial when it comes to fixing their girlfriend's things. And they'll get pissed off if they find out that you've hired another electrician, behind their back, to get the job done. The flipside is that if you don't, your boyfriend might push off getting it done. My advice is to be up-front and firm about the situation. Give him the option to fix it but also give him a timeframe, and be sensitive to his schedule."

Rule #2:

He might not be the most worldly individual.

Though there are some college graduates out there who chose careers as electricians, the majority of these guys start working right after they graduate from high school. "There's definitely a socioeconomic class difference," says Lisa. "My boyfriend hasn't traveled much, hasn't seen much, and he doesn't have that many questions about why the world is the way it is. And while there is something refreshing about how simply he sees things, it can also be frustrating at times. I come from a family of doctors with numerous degrees and occasionally I miss having conversations about art or current affairs or things like that. Still, I have come to realize that there are many types of intelligence. And when I watch my boyfriend dissect and diagnose electrical problems, I realize there's a serious skill there that some of the worldliest individuals don't have."

According to Lauren, a former girlfriend of an electrician, the benefits far outweigh the drawbacks. "You have to ask yourself what you want from a man, and what really matters to you. Is it his character and his values, or is it his cachet? Sure, there were times that I wished my boyfriend and I could have had more intellectual conversations, but I have dated many guys since him and I have yet to find another man that measures up."

Rule #3:

He's not used to being around women.

He spends his days surrounded by other guys, and yes, this will have an effect on his personality. "I constantly hear about my boyfriend's day-to-day antics like using a bucket as a toilet or seeing who can wire up a receptacle the fastest," says Pam. "Since electricians work in predominantly male environments, they don't think twice about watching their language or their manners because there are hardly ever any women around." The good news? You can teach him what is and is not appropriate, and even though he won't apply that to his work life, at least he'll change his attitude when he is at home with you.

Rule #4:
He's incredibly resourceful.

Not only will he fix things around the house, but you'll learn more about household products from this guy than you will from your own mother. "I've never seen anything like it," says Kim. "He's Martha Stewart meets McGyver." Alison agrees. "My ex-boyfriend was the most practical man I ever met. I learned more from him in six months than I did from my lawyer boyfriend of two years. And to be honest, I am still not over him."

So what do these guys know that we don't? Just about everything, from how to prevent tools from rusting by putting a piece of charcoal in the toolbox, to how to drill more easily into concrete using liquid dishwashing detergent. "It's part of the job," says Jeff. "We acquire secret remedies everywhere we go. That piece of charcoal in your toolbox will absorb the moisture caused by condensation. It's the best way to prevent rust and oxidation."

Rule #5:
He won't wear a wedding band to work, ever.

Don't take this personally. It has nothing to do with how he feels about you. These guys cannot wear anything metal to work. "Gold and silver are excellent conductors of electricity," says John. "And any precious metal ring can carry huge currents even at low voltages. And that means that a man's finger could be burned right off his hand." So whatever you do, don't question his loyalty because he can't wear his ring to work. These guys are very safety conscious, and risking that to prove something to you is just not an option.

Rule #6:
Don't expect him to understand what you do all day.

He spends his days climbing up and down ladders, and crouching into small spaces. And when he's not lugging heavy tools and electrical wires, he can be found on a bathroom break at the nearest Porta Potti. Translation? He can't possibly comprehend what you do all day when you leave his apartment in your Marc Jacobs pumps, Theory suit, and Furla handbag. "I was having lunch with the guys one day and they were talking about what a tough morning they had. I agreed with them, mentioning that I too had a tough morning. That's when my boyfriend's friends started laughing at me," says Pam. "One of the guys said, 'what do you know about hard work? All you do is sit at a desk all day and talk on the phone!' And at first I was furious, but then I realized that it had nothing to do with me, and that compared to hanging off a telephone pole all day long in the rain, my job did seem pretty comfortable."

Rule #7:
He's less likely to be threatened by your success.

Sure, these guys might not understand what you do all day, but what boyfriend really does? "He doesn't need to understand," says Lisa, a full-time writer. "Of all the guys I've dated, my electrician boyfriend is by far the most involved in my work. He always wants to read what I write (no other boyfriend did) and he often travels with me to hear me speak or to carry my stuff. He's not threatened by my world or my success. He doesn't feel that he needs to compete with me. And there's something nice about that."

He Says . . .

Give us space when we get home.

"Electricians come home filthy and tired. We need time to clean up, relax, and just zone out. And though it may sound harsh, most of us are probably not in the mood to hear about our girlfriend's problems the minute we get home from work. We are all pretty laid-back, easygoing guys and we need a go-with-the-flow kind of girl." —Kostadinos

We don't make as much money as you think.

"Some girls think that we make a lot of money, but once you consider taxes and paying for our tools and gas and all those little things, we are left with very little. Your guy will most likely have to work weekends taking freelance jobs here and there. Though it might be a pain, it's just part of the job." —Kevin

She Says . . .

Your whole life changes!

"It's amazing. I used to date the lawyers and bankers and now that I am with an electrician it's like a whole new world. And I can't believe it took me this long to figure it out. When we just started dating I was in my new apartment and one of the walls had no electricity and I could never figure it out. When I told him over the phone, his response was, 'I'll be right over with my electric panel.' And truthfully I don't think I've ever been so turned on. Now it's like that every day. Just the other morning he was taking a leak and the toilet wouldn't flush and he was like, 'can you get me my toolbox?' and he fixed the toilet right then and there!" —Lisa

He thinks his way is the only way.

"Don't even think of calling another electrician to do the job or suggesting a second opinion to the problem. My father is an electrician, so is my boyfriend, and they truly think they know the answers to everything. They each have their own way of doing things and they are very set in their ways. My dad used to solve every problem with black electrical tape! The whole house was covered in it and as ridiculous as it was, there was nothing we could do to change his mind." —Stacey

What Kind of Electrician Is He?

There are four specialty areas where you'll find electrical workers. Here's a look at what your electrician might be doing all day.

- **Outside lineman:** He's the guy you see outside working high up on the telephone lines, complete with a hardhat and toolbox. And unlike inside wiremen, this guy has had to develop climbing skills, and spends much of his day atop wooden poles. Though he often works alone (read: he's not around the guys all day), he tends to work in bad weather conditions. Expect him to be outside before, during, and after storms in order to maintain electrical power for homes, hospitals, factories, and schools. Note: He may come home cold, wet, tired, and aggravated.
- **Inside wireman:** These guys install electrical equipment in commercial (e.g., office) and industrial buildings (e.g., power plants and chemical plants)—everything from lighting and receptacles to motors and heating equipment. Expect his days to vary. One day he'll be installing a security system in a high-rise building and the next day he's installing conduit in a ditch on the outside of the building. (Yes, inside wiremen occasionally work outside.)

- **Installer technician:** He installs equipment for everything from telephones and computer networks to video distribution systems, security, and access control systems. Typically this guy works beside the inside wireman, in buildings that are partially or fully enclosed to protect from sun, wind, and rain. Still, these installations are often made before air conditioning, heat, or permanent light fixtures have been installed in the buildings. Translation? He will be working in some pretty uncomfortable conditions.
- **Residential wireman:** Yes, he'll be working in residential homes, and yes, most likely he'll be greeted at the door by a woman, whether she is a housewife, nanny, or housekeeper. But before you freak out, remember, electricians are focused on the task at hand. All it takes is one false move to risk his life and the lives of others. So, relax. Plus, the good news is that residential electricians tend to be more mild-mannered and considerate than installer technicians or outside linemen. Why? They work directly with their clients in the privacy of their homes. Expect him to install anything from energy management systems to security systems to fire alarm systems as well as the standard power distribution systems to lights and receptacles throughout the home.

The Breakdown

Here's a look at the electrician:

biggest turn on	Watching him fix your things
biggest challenge	Getting him to hire someone else
best way to get in touch	On his cell, after work
greatest perk	He knows how to fix things
best timing	Wintertime

Talking Shop

Here's a list of key words and phrases that will help you speak his language:

CAD: No, this has nothing to do with his bachelor status. CAD stands for computer-assisted design, and it's a computer program used to design drawings of electrical systems.

conduit: A fancy word used to mean pipe or tubing. These guys are always installing conduit.

electric shock: No, he's not talking about shock therapy. There is nothing therapeutic about it. Electric shock occurs when a person comes in contact with two conductors of a circuit and the body becomes part of the electrical circuit. A severe shock can cause the heart and lungs to stop functioning.

fault: Before you get all defensive, he's not blaming you for anything. A fault refers to a short circuit in an electrical system.

home runs: This has nothing to do with baseball nor does it have to do with getting to first or second base with a girl. Electricians use the phrase "pulling home runs" to refer to getting the tougher jobs done.

network: No, your guy is not referring to his need to network with other professional electricians. A network refers to a system of transmission lines that are cross-connected to allow for multiple power supply. Note: A network is usually installed in urban areas.

ohm: No, he's not referring to the word we chant in yoga to help us relax. In an electrician's world, the ohm means the unit of measure for resistance.

pothead: It's not what you think. A pothead is a flared, pot-shaped, insulated fitting used to connect underground cables to overhead lines. So now when your guy says "I used a pothead today," at least you'll know what he's talking about.

trip out: Again, this has nothing to do with drugs! A trip out means nothing other than the fact that there was a disconnection of an electric circuit. When a line "trips out," the circuit breaker has opened and the line is out of service.

chapter 12 The Automotive Technician

(the artist formerly known as "the Mechanic")

He's that guy working on your car in the back room of the dealership. And while you anxiously wait to hear the dreaded estimate on your car repairs, you find yourself oddly comforted by the fact that this guy is working on your car. You watch him from a distance as he opens your hood and examines the engine before disappearing underneath the car for further inspection. And even though the two of you have never spoken, or even made eye contact, you feel as though you could observe this guy for hours. Maybe it's the confidence he exudes when he handles all that machinery, or perhaps it's the fact that he is, in an indirect, yet irresistible way, taking care of you. You find yourself hoping that he'll be the one to make his way to the front of the shop to talk with you about next steps. Sadly, this never happens. In fact, the minute he's done working on your car he disappears from your view. So, who is this guy? And could he actually be as attentive to you as he was to your vehicle?

His Look

Filthy, in that boys will be boys sort of way. Still, there's something very cute about this guy. Almost like he's living out his childhood fantasy. Expect his uniform (dark blue pants, solid blue shirt, and workboots) to be covered in grease stains. In fact, you'll be lucky if you can make out his name embroidered on his front pocket. These guys don't get the nickname grease monkey for no reason, and he'll almost always be dirty at work. At home, though, he's known to clean up quite nicely (minus his poor fingernails, which will never, ever be completely clean).

His Vibe

Quiet and focused, at least when he's busy working. Remember, most technicians don't interact with customers. Instead, they're in the back of the shop, checking under the hood or lying on the ground, hard at work underneath a car. Expect this guy to be incredibly focused when he's diagnosing a mechanical problem. He takes his work very seriously. In fact, technicians have been known to compare themselves to doctors, and literally think about cars the way doctors think about their patients. Note: Unlike construction workers, these guys don't spend their lunch break talking about women. They spend them trading war stories about the various cars they've worked on.

His Hours

Those who work in auto dealerships have set hours of 8 A.M. to 5 P.M., five days a week. Guys who work in the repair shops and gas stations have less predictable schedules, which can include late nights and busy Saturdays. Note: Regardless of his schedule, most technicians choose to work weekend jobs, just to make extra cash.

Risk Factor

Though it sounds harsh, he may in fact care about cars more than he cares about you. Some of these guys are so obsessed with cars that it's all they talk about. When they're not at work they can be found attending car shows, surfing the Internet for car sites, building model cars, and upgrading the engine on their vintage Mustang convertible.

Perks

He's project-oriented, detailed, and incredibly handy. He'll change your flat tire, fix your brakes, replace your engine . . . he'll even install video monitors and upgrade your sound system. Though the median hourly income is $18.37, master technicians (technicians with all eight certifications) can earn from $70,000 to $100,000 a year.

Will You Rule Him Out?

Before you decide, here's a look at what to expect when you are dating an automotive technician.

Rule #1:
These guys aren't just uneducated grease monkeys.

For starters the term "car mechanic" is no longer politically correct. He's a skilled automotive technician. Got it? Good. 'Cause that's not the only difference. Today's technicians are extensively trained and specialized. And most of them have at least one certification. (Getting certified typically involves two years of courses followed by a written exam.) "Now that 80 percent of cars are computerized, there's a lot more to this job than traditional hand tools," says Daniel. "Technicians have to understand wiring and schematics. Most new cars have multiple onboard computers controlling everything from the engine to the radio. And it's our job to know how these things work, what went wrong, how it went wrong, and how to fix it."

Rule #2:
Don't call him at work unless it's important.

Every time he gets a phone call, someone from the shop screams out his name and tells him to stop what he's working on and come take the call. So unless you want every guy in his shop to know how many times you call your boyfriend in a given day, chances are you should wait until he gets home. Also, don't forget that these guys get paid according to the amount of work they do, which means the more times he has to get out from under that car to take your phone calls, the less he's going to fix, and therefore make. Plus technicians are incredibly focused when they're at work; their job is to literally examine a car's parts to find out what's not working and how to fix it. One phone call could break his concentration and cost him another hour of inspection. So before you pick up that phone just to say hi, ask yourself, *is this really necessary*?

Rule #3:
This guy's either completely obsessed with cars or he wants nothing to do with them the minute he leaves the shop.

Though some guys hate working on their own cars because they spend their entire day working on everyone else's car, other guys simply can't get enough. The good news is that you should be able to tell which guy you're dating right off the bat. How will you know? The obsessed ones can't keep it a secret for more than ten minutes. "We sat down for dinner, and before we even got the menus he was bringing up some amazing story about a car he repaired," says Jen. "It was literally the only time his face lit up the entire meal." Hopefully you will find this innocent and endearing. "I've gotten used to this because I love him, and I keep telling myself that it's not like he's obsessed with women or addicted to drugs or anything. It's just cars," says Sara. "Still, some days I just want to sell the damn thing. He's always working on that Mustang. And when he's not in the garage, he's watching his twenty car shows on TV or he's surfing the Web reading about cars. Do you know that they even have car clubs?"

Rule #4:
If he can't fix something it will drive him crazy.

This guy's a problem solver, which means he won't give up on something without testing out every possible scenario. Though he's typically patient with everything, including you, he can also become extremely frustrated when something that seems so simple isn't working the way it should. "There are times when I literally have to cancel our dinner plans because he refuses to walk away from a car he's working on. And the reality is that even if I got him to walk away for a little bit, it still wouldn't be worth it because he'd be sitting at dinner trying to figure out what the problem was in his head." The good news is that most of these guys approach life the way they approach cars. "They are some of the most dedicated, diligent guys I know," says Stacey. "And when I need my boyfriend to fix something, whether it's my computer or the cabinet in my bathroom, he never complains. And he never puts it off either, no matter how tired he is."

Rule #5:
He will take odd jobs after work and on the weekends.

This is inevitable, since many of these guys make twice as much money working freelance jobs than they do at their regular gigs. "This drives my girlfriend crazy," says Daniel, "especially when the jobs I take are on the weekends. I try to explain to her that I can make a couple hundred bucks in a few hours this way. Still, sometimes she doesn't seem to get it, and feels like I am choosing work over her. Whatever you do, try not to get pissed at your boyfriend if he works weekends, even if he's working at a friend's repair shop. Every technician that wants to move up has to work other jobs to learn more, and to make more money, especially if he wants to do more than fix cars. Fixing cars is my day job, but really I am an electronic troubleshooter who works on everything from trains to go-carts."

Rule #6:
He may come home sore, bruised, and frustrated.

Unlike guys with desk jobs (i.e., lawyers and bankers), technicians spend their days squeezing into tight spaces, maintaining uncomfortable positions for hours at a time. Plus they work with everything from heavy and dangerous welding equipment to massive power drills so it's not uncommon for them to come home with burns or pretty nasty bruises. "We are constantly cutting the tips of our fingers or stabbing them with sharp tools," says Steve. "Plus we need to follow all this protocol: gloves, goggles, ear plugs, and no jewelry. So, don't get pissed at your guy when he won't wear that necklace or ring you gave him to work. It has nothing to do with wearing it in front of the guys and everything to do with the fact that it could melt or get caught in one of the machines." As for your guy's work frustrations, these can be caused by any number of reasons. "If he loses one of his tools, he's bound to get pissed off," says Steve. "Those tools are really expensive and many of us have to buy them ourselves. Also, we might be working on a car for hours only to realize that the problem was something else entirely, like an electrical problem. Knowing that we could have fixed the thing hours ago is really frustrating. Also, occasionally we'll be working on one problem area of a car and just when we start to fix it, something else breaks. That's the worst because you can't bill someone for something that you break."

Rule #7:

Fifteen minutes really means an hour.

He will get completely lost in his work and lose track of time. "This happens to me all the time," says Dave. "My girlfriend will ask me when I'll be home for dinner and I'll say fifteen minutes and literally an hour later I walk in and she's pissed and the food is cold and she's already eaten alone. The problem is that we get so focused on a specific car and we have no concept of time. We might think we can fix something in ten minutes but then it's not always that easy. And at that point, ten minutes has gone by, but we are already so entrenched in our work that we forget everything around us! Plus in our defense, we don't wear watches when we are working." So what should you do when this happens? "My advice is to literally add forty-five minutes to everything your guy says," says Daniel. "That way if he says he'll be back in fifteen minutes and he returns an hour later, you are right on schedule."

What's His Specialty?

Gone are the days of general auto mechanics! Now most guys have to be specialized in at least one area. Here's a look at what kind of technician you might be dating.

- **Transmission technician:** He works on (duh) transmissions. Chances are he'll talk about everything from gear trains to hydraulic pumps. Since most transmissions are highly computerized, this guy will have to be able to fix various computer controls and any potential electrical and hydraulic problems. Transmission technicians work with some of the most sophisticated technology used in cars.
- **Tune-up technician:** This guy spends his days adjusting the ignition or replacing spark plugs. His job is to make sure that the engine is performing efficiently. Though he will use his share of traditional hand tools, he tends to rely on electronic testing equipment to first isolate and then adjust any malfunctions in fuel, ignition, and emissions systems.
- **Automotive air-conditioning repairer:** He handles anything AC-related, which includes the installation and repair of every component of the AC unit from

the compressors and condensers to the controls. Note: These workers require special training in federal and state regulations governing the handling and disposal of refrigerants.

- **Front-end mechanic:** He spends much of his time repairing steering mechanics and suspension systems, as well as aligning and balancing wheels. Front-end mechanics tend to use special alignment equipment and wheel balancing machines.
- **Brake repairer:** These guys adjust brakes, replace brake linings and pads, and make other repairs on brake systems. Some technicians and mechanics specialize in both brake and front-end work.

He Says . . .

Your guy will grow out of his car obsession.

"Most mechanics grew up around cars and yes, we have that whole boyish fantasy with cars but the older I got, the more my car obsession faded. At seventeen, I was thrilled to be working in my first shop. I felt like the epitome of a man. But as I continued working in shops and getting older, I began to care less and even started to let other people work on my cars. Now the last thing I want to do is come home and work on my car. Be patient with your guy—he may seem obsessed now, but he'll grow out of it."—Dave

Find out if he wears his uniform after hours.

"Some guys love to flaunt what they do and they get a charge out of people coming up to them and asking for help on their car. Not me. I always shower and change at work because the last thing I want is for people in my neighborhood to realize that I am a technician and then start asking me if I'll just take a look at their car for a second. I don't want to work on people's cars after work and so I try to keep things completely separate. Find out what kind of guy your guy is before you judge him. And if he's one of those guys that wants to be Mr. Fix-It 24/7, ask yourself if you can live with that."—Daniel

She Says . . .

Once you get into it, this stuff is fun.

"It's easy to hate something when you're not included! At first all his projects annoyed me, but then he started to teach me about cars, and I learned everything from welding to replacing engines. After I mastered welding, he gave me some spare parts and our old lawn mower, and I built myself a go-cart! It was pretty cool. I started rebuilding a ten-year-old Chevy, and I turned it into a fast car. My best advice would be to get involved in the things he loves. The worst thing you can do is complain about it for the sake of complaining. Plus, it's not like you're dealing with a drunk or drug addict. He's just simply addicted to cars which, in the grand scheme of things, isn't all that bad."—Melissa

He takes his job seriously

"He really does think of himself as a doctor so try to understand the importance of his job, or at least the fact that it's important to him. One time I was pissed that he wasn't home on time and he said, 'you wouldn't expect me to leave a dying patient on the examining table, would you?' I almost burst out laughing but I knew that he was serious and it was actually pretty endearing. Just remember that he takes pride in what he does and is super responsible, which is actually a really good thing."—Kate

The Breakdown

Here's the skinny on the automotive technician:

biggest turn on	Watching him fix your car
biggest challenge	Getting him to stop working
best way to get in touch	On his cell, after work
greatest perk	He can fix anything
best timing	Dinnertime

Talking Shop

Here's a list of key words and phrases that will help you speak his language:

Bead seat: No, it's not that weird-looking seat cushion that taxi drivers use for their back! The bead seat is the inner portion on the wheel rim.

Bleeding: Though he may be referring to an on-the-job injury, he could be referring to the term as it relates to the purging of air from a brake system. Find out before you unnecessarily freak out.

Dipstick: No, he's not using sixth-grade insults again, at least not when he refers to the dipstick. A dipstick is actually a thin metal rod, which is inserted into the oil reservoir to measure how much oil is left in the engine. Dipsticks are also used to check the transmission fluid.

Idiot light: A derogatory term that refers to the warning light on an instrument panel (it might signal that the gas tank is almost empty, or the washer fluid is out). It's used to catch the driver's attention when they are close to the danger zone.

Lube job: The lubrication of a suspension system. This sounds sexier than it is.

Manual transmission: Commonly referred to as stick shift. Unlike automatic transmission, which is (duh!) automatic, manual transmission is manual and therefore the driver has to change gears using a hand-operated gearshift and foot-operated clutch. All auto mechanics should know how to drive this way. If he really likes you, he will teach you how to drive this way too.

Shrinkage: The shrinking of an automotive paint as it dries.

part 4:
Men in Uniform

"Sure, I knew he was adorable in his uniform, but that was the only way I'd seen him. I have to admit that I was nervous before our first date. Every time I was at the firehouse there was always this PT Cruiser parked out front and it was purple with yellow flames down the side. So at first I thought, 'Oh god, what if that's his car?!' And since I had no idea what he looked like in normal clothes, I couldn't help but wonder what kind of style a guy with a PT Cruiser would actually have. Derrick and I had a good laugh about that a few months later."—Antonia

the lowdown

his job	personality traits	most commonly used gadget	how he spends his weekends	his biggest concern
fireman	charismatic, brave, loyal	his car	washing his car	survival
military	dedicated, professional, patriotic	firearms	training	survival
airline pilot	confident, romantic	airplane	flying	passenger safety

chapter 13

The Fireman

He's incredibly sexy in that uniform, and when he smiles at you from his big red truck you can't help but feel a little flushed. This guy is the poster boy for everything masculine. He's strong, brave, confident, and caring. Plus, he's dedicated his life to saving others, and what could be sexier than that? Add to that the fact that firemen are also friendly, outgoing, and often genuinely happy individuals who—get this—actually love their jobs! When you walk by the firehouse he tells you to stop by the fireman's fundraiser later that afternoon. It's a softball tournament and he needs someone to cheer for him on the sidelines. He has such a twinkle in his eyes when he says it that you can't resist. Later that evening you take a seat in the bleachers next to all the other girlfriends and wives, and you cheer him on, feeling like you are part of some camp color war. By the end of the night you've met all the guys from the firehouse and you have six more invitations for birthday parties, BBQ's, and fundraisers that week.

His Look

Brave, confident (some are more cocky than others), caring, and heroic. Most of these guys are clean-cut with short hair, and it doesn't hurt that they're also in phenomenal shape. Firefighters have to go through a gruesome physical training process and workouts are part of their daily routine. When he's in uniform expect him to act a bit more assertive and confident. Firefighters love their jobs and they're incredibly proud of what they do. Note: These guys are obsessed with their cars, so expect him to spend the majority of his free time talking about it, driving it, or washing it (he wouldn't be caught dead at a car wash). As for the car he drives, it's typically a pickup truck or an SUV.

His Vibe

Funny, playful, responsible, caring, and courageous. When they're not putting out fires or responding to calls, chances are they're working out, watching sports together, attending a fundraising event, or washing their cars. Different firehouses, and even different shifts, have distinctive vibes. Some firehouses are like frat houses, with single guys, huge egos, and lots of partying. Others are filled with committed, devoted family men. Regardless of what kind of firehouse it is, these guys all have a boys' club mentality (there's a lot of camaraderie) and firehouses are filled with La-Z-Boy recliners and large-screen TVs. Though firemen might be known for having a few drinks after work, make no mistake, they are under tight supervision. Don't be surprised if he has to take the occasional polygraph or drug test. It's pretty standard given the amount of responsibility he has.

His Hours

Though he works long hours (these guys work many overnights), he also has substantial time off in between shifts. A regular schedule typically consists of twenty-four-hour days ten days out of the month, including weekends and holidays. Some cities have firefighters on a day shift of ten hours for three or four days (meaning they will come home to you at night), and then a night shift of fourteen hours for three or four nights (AKA, "girls' night out"), with three or four days off in between. Regardless of the way his schedule is mapped out, firefighters should know which days they are working a year in advance, so there should be no surprises. If he's working nights, expect him to sleep at the firehouse with the rest of the guys. This could happen as often as three times a week. Note: In order to be a firefighter this guy has to go through a number of exams, both physical and written, so don't expect him to be as available when he's preparing for one of these.

Risk Factor

They put their lives on the line every day. And though they might not come home physically injured, chances are they'll come home mentally drained. Firefighters are exposed to a lot of tragedy. They are confronted with new situations every day, and they see a lot of people who have lost loved ones. Don't be surprised if your handsome, courageous, broad-shouldered boyfriend comes home feeling emotionally deflated. This can be an incredibly demanding job, and certain days are worse than others.

Perks

He looks phenomenal in his uniform, he's in great physical shape, he knows CPR, and he's great around the house. Firemen can cook and clean (in the firehouse they take turns cleaning the bathrooms, cooking dinner, taking out the trash, etc.), and they know how to fix everything around the house (including a flat tire). Plus, he has a predictable schedule! Though he may work long hours, his schedule is condensed into fixed blocks of time. What does this mean for you? Most likely he'll have plenty of time to spend with you, and your hypothetical kids. These guys also get great benefits (and an excellent retirement plan) and it seems that everywhere they go they get discounts on everything from TVs and cars to home appliances, electronics, dinners, mattresses, you name it. Note: Captains make six-figure salaries.

Chain of Command

What do those titles really mean?

- **Chief officer:** This guy is responsible for the general management and the day-to-day operations, including the maintenance of the fire trucks and their equipment (making sure everything is operating well and ready in the event of a fire). The fire chief is the first chief officer in the chain of command. He has the ultimate responsibility and is the primary representative at the scene of any incident.
- **Deputy fire chief:** In the event of the chief officer's absence, the deputy fire chief would take over this role, followed by the assistant fire chief.
- **Captains:** Captains report to the fire chief in command.
- **Vehicle captains:** These guys are responsible for the maintenance of their vehicles as well as the equipment on them. They are also responsible for the training and testing of the drivers and operators of the vehicles.

Will You Rule Him Out?

Rule #1:

Firefighters treat their cars the way investment bankers treat their BlackBerry.

Don't feel bad if he stares at his car more than he stares at you. According to a number of girlfriends, a firefighter's car is his number one baby and he will check on it numerous times a day. It's also his favorite topic of conversation. Though you might think these guys sit around and talk about women all day, the reality is that they would much rather talk about a particular wiper fluid or a new waxing technique. Just as most investment bankers wouldn't be caught outside the house without their BlackBerry, most firefighters wouldn't be caught outside the house without their pickup truck or SUV. And when they're not in their car, they can be found washing their car.

Rule #2:

Don't let him know how much you worry.

You have to trust that he knows what he is doing and that he's trained really well. "In the beginning if I didn't hear from my boyfriend by a certain time, I would freak out," says Meredith. "But when I mentioned this to one of the other firefighter's girlfriends, she told me that I should never let him know that I'm afraid, because it could distract him. A firefighter needs to be completely focused on his job and if he's thinking about you when he runs into a burning building, he might be more tentative. And that slight hesitation could make a huge difference. My advice is to become friends with other firefighter's wives. When I get nervous, I call the other women."

Rule #3:
Don't call the firehouse too much or else the guys will make fun of him.

Unless you really need him for something, the best thing to do is to give him space to do his job. Though firefighters have cell phones, often cell phones don't work in the firehouse. Each house has one department line, and you're not encouraged to tie that up with personal phone calls. Call your guy too many times and he's going to become the laughingstock of the house. So what should you expect when he's on a twenty-four-hour shift? "He should call you at night, before he goes to bed, but not much more than that," says Kelly. "It's not that he doesn't care about you or how your day was; it's just that it's not that easy for him to make personal calls. The department line is for emergency calls, not for casual conversations."

Rule #4:
If something bad happens at work, chances are he'll turn to the guys before he turns to you.

This can be very hard for girlfriends to understand. When a woman has a problem at work, she wants to talk to her boyfriend. When a guy has a problem, he wants to talk to the guys. Firefighters have a whole brotherhood thing going on and the bond is very strong, so don't be offended if you are not the first person he comes to. This is a very emotional job and no one understands the stresses better than a fellow firefighter. Still, there are times when he'll need your additional support and he will expect you to be there. "The first time I ever saw my boyfriend really affected by a call was when an old man barreled through the Santa Monica Farmers' Market and killed a lot of men, women, and children. He told me that he saw mangled strollers and dead children, and he just felt like he was going to lose it," says Antonia. "You have to be open to listening to some very tragic stories, no matter how scary they may be."

Rule #5:
You will spend nights sleeping alone and yes, he will have to work some weekends and major holidays.

Though you might be off on the weekends, your firefighter boyfriend could be on duty both nights, and that means no dinner dates, parties, or cozy nights in, sleeping in bed together. He might also be scheduled to work Christmas Day or Thanksgiving, which he is stuck with unless another firefighter wants to switch shifts with him. The good news is that these guys get their schedule a year in advance, so you should have plenty of time to plan ahead.

Rule #6:
He will act more confident when he's in uniform.

Expect a noticeable difference in his personality when he's suited up in uniform. Being a fireman is certainly something to be proud of, and most of these guys feel very confident when they're on the job. "A friend of my fiancé joked with me that Derek never would have had the nerve to approach me and ask me out if he hadn't been in his uniform. And now that I've been with him for so long, I'd have to agree. It's kind of cute actually, and I don't blame him. Even I act different when he's in uniform. It's just this amazing sense of pride that you have seeing these guys, your guy in particular, all suited up and ready for anything or anyone who needs them," says Antonia.

Rule #7:

When you date a fireman, you take on more than just a boyfriend; it's an entire lifestyle.

Get ready for picnics, barbecues, softball tournaments, endless fundraisers, and a brotherhood bond that no one can tear down. Your guy will be incredibly close with the other firemen. After all, they practically live together and they depend on one another to save lives. Firefighters love to be active and they love being active together, so get ready to welcome an entire community of new friends. Why? Because firemen are very loyal individuals, and they will be there for one another in any time of need, no questions asked. "So, get used to sharing your man, even when he is not working," says Kelly. "Don't get me wrong, there are plenty of perks to this as well. Like, if we're putting up a fence at the house or building something, they always show up to pitch in. I'll be in the middle of carrying something heavy and five guys will come up and take it from me. It's really a big family, and being the girlfriend or wife of a firefighter means embracing that."

The Breakdown

Here's the dish on the fireman:

biggest turn on	He saves lives
biggest challenge	Dealing with the fact that he's risking his life
best way to get in touch	Let him call you
greatest perk	He has a predictable schedule with flexibility
best timing	In between shifts

He Says . . .

We understand that you would rather we have a safer job, just as long as you understand that it's never going to happen.

"Most of us have wanted to be firemen since we were little. This is not a career you just jump into because you think it sounds cool, and it's not a career that you can walk away from easily. My father was a fireman, as was my stepfather, and everything I did as a kid, including college, was to prepare for this. There's also a lot of training that's involved, physical, psychological, and book work. This is a lifestyle choice and most of us are incredibly passionate about what we do. I love that not every day is exactly like the day before. It's the most empowering, rewarding feeling to save someone's life, and there is an incredible rush and thrill that comes with a fireman's everyday duties."—Derek

We need a woman who's independent and strong.

"Our jobs require us to be away sometimes two or three nights a week, and we need to know that you'll be okay with that. It's a drawback for a lot of women, but there are so many pluses to our career that it really does even out. Like when we're off duty, we have so much flexibility, which allows us to be very involved with our families. A lot of the guys here take their kids to soccer games and get them off to school in the morning—when they're not on duty, of course. Still, like with any job, there are drawbacks. We may be stuck working Christmas day, Thanksgiving, or the weekend of your birthday, and even though we can try to buddy up with a few guys to change around our schedule, nothing's guaranteed."—Jeff

Don't expect us to be able to run home in the middle of the day to fix the toaster.

"It's not like a nine-to-five desk job. We can't meet you for lunch in the middle of the day or run home to fix something that broke. We have to be ready at all times for anything that might occur."—Rich

We go through intensive training to become firefighters.

"A lot of women don't realize all the training that's involved. We have to take a written exam, an oral exam, and complete six months of intensive fire academy training, which includes learning basic firefighting, emergency medical training, technical rescue training, working with hazardous materials, etc. Plus, there are always fire drills and terrorism drills. The first year is the most overwhelming. And no matter how bad your guy wanted to be a firefighter, he never could have anticipated what he was in for. Also, expect your guy to be hazed a bit in the beginning. He's a probie, which means that on top of all the stress of being new on the job, he'll have to do all the grunt work in the house, like clean the toilets, cook, wash the dishes, and make sure all the masks are on the truck, things like that."—Mike

She Says . . .

Some people think firemen drink a lot and cheat on their wives.

"There are idiots in every profession, and yes, some firehouses have bad reputations, but overall, the firemen I know are some of the most devoted, loyal, decent people I've ever met. I think the single guys play hard, but once they settle down they are really devoted family men. So, if you're really worried about him cheating on you, spend time at his firehouse and see what kind of place it is. He doesn't have much control over which firehouse he's in, but if he works his connections, he can put in for a transfer."—Kate

Get used to being alone some nights, weekends, and holidays.

"Overall, they have great schedules with flexible hours, but inevitably they will be scheduled to work on a major holiday or event. That's just the way it goes, and unless he can find someone to trade with, you're out of luck. Yes, this includes Christmas day, your birthday, anniversaries, Easter, Thanksgiving, you name it. The good news is that his work schedule is determined a year in advance, so at least you'll have time to deal with it!"—Antonia

He may be out of contact for days.

"My boyfriend has had to work on brush fires where he'd be gone for several days and I'd have little or no contact with him. Sometimes he's had to set up camp in deserted locations and work twelve-hour shifts at a time. Or if there is a disaster in another country such as an earthquake, flooding, structure collapse, his team might be dispatched to go and find the survivors in all the rubble. It's not easy when you have no contact. In fact, it sucks, but you kind of just have to deal with it. Remember that he's been well trained, he's had numerous terrorism drills and fire drills, and he knows what he's doing. And remember, they always say that no news is good news. In other words, if something bad happens, you are going to know about it."—Karen

Talking Shop

Here's a list of key words and phrases that will help you speak his language:

Bunker gear: The protective clothing worn by firefighters, including helmets, truck belts, radio straps, and leather boots.

Bus: Ambulances are often referred to as buses or wagons.

Captains: Leader of the crew. Captains are in charge of the overall welfare and safety of their crew, training of firefighters, scene control, and devising plans/tactics for all emergency responses.

Chief deputies: The guys who are in charge of either operations or administration (there are two of them in each firehouse).

Code 4: A code firemen commonly use to announce that a situation is under control.

Engineers: These are the guys in charge of driving the truck, maintaining the truck, setting up water nozzles and gauging water supply for fires, fire equipment, roof operations, and ladder placement for burning buildings. Engineers do not go into burning buildings.

Fire chief: The person in charge of policy and administration within the department; also serves as a liaison between county supervisors and the fire department.

Firefighters: Their responsibilities include responding to medical calls in addition to fighting fires; most firefighters are trained as paramedics.

Forward lay: A technique in which hose lines are laid from a fire hydrant to the fire scene, usually being pulled from the hose bed as the engine drives forward.

Frequent flyer: Though firefighters take care of many emergency situations, they also get calls on a number of minor issues. A frequent flyer is the term firefighters give to individuals who repeatedly call 911 for minor issues.

House dues: Money collected by the firefighters to pay for food, cable, phone, computer/Internet and any other extras the guys want to have in their station.

Reverse lay: Laying hose from the fire scene back to a water source, such as a fire hydrant.

chapter 14 The Military Guy

You remember the ROTC guy you couldn't help but notice on campus all throughout your college days? He seemed so much more mature than the other college boys who spent their downtime playing drinking games at the fraternity house. This guy was different. He had a purpose, plus there was something so sexy about watching him run drills in his camouflage uniform. Part of you found him mysterious; you couldn't help but wonder what made this guy so motivated and fearless. The other part of you found him intimidating. After all, what's so noble about you pursuing a career in fashion when people like him risk their lives to serve our country? Regardless, the two of you eventually crossed paths (you made sure of it) and when you did, you introduced yourself. He seemed so official, so respectful, and so damn cute. And within weeks of dating him you were completely smitten. Unfortunately, you were also in for a huge awakening, because once he left college he went off to serve his country. The question is, why didn't you go with him?

His Look

Clean-cut (yes, he will have short hair), professional, and respectful. Expect him to act more serious when he's in uniform, even when he's not on duty. Serving in the military is an honor, and with that honor comes certain responsibilities. When he's out of uniform and off base, however, he'll be much more casual and relaxed. As serious as they are on base, these guys like to party and have fun. As for his sense of style, he doesn't really have one. Expect him to adapt to the style of whatever state he is stationed in (for example, guys stationed in Texas will wear cowboy boots).

His Vibe

On base everyone in the military is extremely polite, respectful, and motivated. The atmosphere is professional, straightforward, and very business oriented, and these guys are typically very organized and diligent, regardless of their rank. Though the young enlisted ones are known to be less educated and a bit rough around the edges (most of them came straight out of high school), they are still thought to be more dedicated and responsible than your average seventeen-year-old civilian. Expect your guy to be responsible, respectful (he is taught to respect the chain of command), proud, confident, and in control. When he's out of uniform, expect him to seem much more relaxed and outgoing. When he's not out partying with the guys, he can be found doing something active outdoors—anything from hunting to white-water rafting, mountain climbing, motorcycling . . . you name it!

Risk Factor

It depends on where he's stationed, what his position is, and whether he's enlisted, an officer, or in the reserves. While Marines and sailors can be deployed for six months at a time with a high probability of being in an area of combat, for others like those in the U.S. Air Force, it is highly unlikely. Military life can be very isolating and lonely, especially at the beginning. If your guy has just gone in for active duty, expect him to get sent to remote places where he doesn't know a soul.

Perks

He's in great shape (he has to work out several days a week and pass monthly fitness tests). He's loyal, proud of what he does, and capable of handling almost any situation, which means you'll always feel safe when you're around him. As for his living expenses, they're next to nothing. His meals are taken care of, he has substantial tax advantages, free memberships, and incredible deals on everything from clothes to food. Plus, he has access to special travel packages, hotels, and airline fares for up to 75 percent off. Oh, and he gets free medical insurance for everyone in his family and a great retirement plan after twenty years.

Badge of Honor

Want to know what his title really means?

- **Second lieutenant:** Most commonly addressed as "Lieutenant," the second lieutenant is the entry-level rank for most commissioned officers.
- **First lieutenant:** Also addressed as "Lieutenant," the first lieutenant is more seasoned (known as a senior lieutenant). He leads more specialized weapons platoons and is often selected to be the executive officer of a company-sized unit.
- **Captain:** Addressed as "Captain," he commands and controls company-sized units of up to 200 soldiers. In addition, captains serve as instructors at combat training centers.
- **Colonel:** The colonel typically commands battalion-sized units (300 to 1,000 soldiers).
- **Brigadier general:** Addressed as "General," this guy has one star on his right lapel. He serves as deputy commander and assists in overseeing the staff's planning and coordination of a mission.
- **Major general:** Also addressed as "General," he has two stars on his right lapel. He typically commands division-sized units of up to 15,000 soldiers.

Will You Rule Him Out?

Before you decide, here's a look at what to expect when you're dating a guy in the military.

Rule #1:

He may seem different when he's in uniform.

Expect him to act differently when he's in uniform. Chances are he will be more polite, straightforward, and business-like. He will also exude greater confidence and authority. "I've noticed that people are a lot nicer to us when he's in his uniform," says Sara. "A lot of people nod their heads in respect; little kids like to wave and ask if he has a gun. Some people even appear a little nervous, which I always find funny. I don't know how it is for other areas, but in the Air Force they have certain rules when he's in uniform. For example, they strongly discourage any public displays of affection, which means my boyfriend can only give me a peck on the cheek and no lengthy hugs. That can be incredibly frustrating, especially when we haven't seen each other in a while."

Rule #2:

These guys have their lives planned out and many of them want to get married early.

By the time cadets are seniors in college they get anxious to have their lives figured out. This is when they have to put in a request for what base/post and job they want, which also includes the dreaded question, is anyone coming with you (if you bring a girlfriend, fiancée, or wife, you are entitled to a higher stipend for living expenses). "I had just turned twenty-one and my boyfriend expected me to decide right then and there if I wanted to live with him next year," says Charlotte. "The Air Force makes you plan your life out long term, and my boyfriend had a hard time understanding that this sort of rationale is not normal for the rest of us. It's this system of forms and boxes, like, 'Wife? Check this box.' He checks a box and suddenly I live with him for free! That's the mentality, and it's so easy and logical to them. I check a box and my entire life changes. I move across the country and leave everyone and everything I've established for myself behind. This has been a sore point for us, and I still don't know if I can just check a box and uproot my life."

Rule #3:
This guy is not a game player.

There are no shades of gray with this guy. What you see is what you get, and most likely this guy's willing to put it all out there for you with a sort of take it or leave it mentality. Why? Because he doesn't have the time or the energy to play games. Plus, it's not in his nature. If he likes you, you'll know it, and if he's serious about you, you'll know that too. That's not to say that these guys don't like to hook up with women for the sake of hooking up (have you met a young enlisted guy?), but it does mean that if he's serious about you, he will tell you. Military guys are straightforward and bold. They're also very loyal and they always stand up for what they believe in. After all, they put their lives on the line each and every day to serve their country. So, what does this mean for you? You'll always know where you stand with him. However, if he likes you, you better start thinking about what you want from him, because he's going to want to move things forward. These guys tend to settle down much earlier than the average lawyer or investment banker.

Rule #4:
These guys are very traditional in their views about women.

Many of them will have a hard time understanding why their girlfriend would choose a career over joining them while they are on active duty. In fact, it's almost expected that if this guy is serious about a woman she will put her career goals on hold to be with him. "I don't know how it is now, but ten years ago officers' wives were pretty much told to be housewives. I am sure it's changed a little, but they are definitely behind the times," says Connie. According to Sara it hasn't changed that much: "I am graduating college this year and I want to pursue a career in PR, but he doesn't understand why. He just doesn't understand that working in PR requires hands-on experience. It's not like a business or finance degree, where you have the skills and you just go apply whenever. I don't want to be applying for an internship or entry-level job for the first time at twenty-five, and that is absolutely foreign to him, coming from a system where you follow the requirements and everything just works like clockwork. It can be frustrating when their entire life is mapped out for them and you have to figure yours out along the way. He just expects my life to be set. I think it's because the marriage age in the military is so young. My theory is that the majority of people in the armed forces come from small towns where it's common to settle down early, and the women usually take on the roles of housewife and mother."

Rule #5:
There's a big difference between the guys who enlist in the military and those who go through an ROTC program in college and then go on to become officers.

Being enlisted means that you could be called at any time to go work on a base or post for a few months. You can enlist immediately while in high school, and you get into the system a lot quicker than if you do ROTC and active duty, but the pay and level of job importance is ultimately a lot less. A guy who's enlisted might get called to a base or post where he doesn't know anyone, and he'll get put up in a one-bedroom apartment and get stuck doing some mundane activity. He might be guarding the base or post, or cooking food in the cafeteria, or driving a truck. Regardless, a lot of times his hours are weird, the job is far from rewarding, and there's a lot of time spent alone. All too often these guys get lonely and feel isolated, and many of them have been known to drink a lot when they're off duty. "When I think of those guys—and some of them are friends with my boyfriend—I think of each of them finishing off an entire bottle of hard liquor by themselves on a Tuesday night. It's kind of scary," says Meredith.

Rule #6:
Don't expect him to check in often when he's training.

Those first few months of active duty are very demanding and overwhelming, so don't expect your guy to be checking in all the time. Chances are he's traveling from one base/post to the next, training with a group of people he doesn't know, in an area where he's never been. Claire's military boyfriend travels a lot, and she says, "They don't get a lot of warning before they have to leave, either. My boyfriend just went active duty, and he's been traveling all the time. One time I was prepared to meet him somewhere for the weekend and he had to call me at the last minute to say that they had sent him to Birmingham for six weeks. It's hard to get used to, but it's also hard for them. It's really lonely in the beginning since they don't know anyone."

Rule #7:
If there's a woman in his detachment or at a training session, expect him to work closely with her for long hours.

There's a frequent wave of groups that get put on active duty or sent to training at one time, and every few weeks a new group rolls in. This means that when your boyfriend is new, about fourteen other people are too. Yes, there will be a few women in that group, and yes, he will wind up hanging out with them a lot because they won't know anyone else. Get used to this. They'll have to train together and work closely with one another. And when he's in training, his downtime is spent on base, usually in some crappy, middle-of-nowhere town, so these people are kind of forced to bond and keep each other entertained. Yikes!

He Says . . .

If you meet a guy in college and he's a cadet in the ROTC, he will be serving in the military for at least a few years.

"It doesn't really sink in for a lot of women. For some reason they don't really think you'll be leaving for the military after college. It's like they know that you have all these requirements when you are in school together and that you walk around in your uniform, but it doesn't hit them that you will be leaving them after senior year. Try to come to terms with this because once a guy becomes a cadet and goes into the ROTC, he is committing himself to four years of service. And at that point if you are still together, he will probably want you to go with him."—Michael

Many of us will pursue other careers after a few years.

"The average guy stays in the military for four years and then seeks out another profession. Sure, there are guys that choose to make a career out of it, but there are plenty of guys that become lawyers, pilots, businessmen. . . . Find out what your boyfriend's plan is before you assume he's in the military for life."—Josh

She Says . . .

Don't be afraid to complain to him.

"So many people ask me if I feel bad complaining about my day-to-day life when my boyfriend is out there representing our country. The truth is that I don't feel guilty by any means, because he chose this career and it is something he was interested in. I think he also likes to hear my day-to-day because it puts things in perspective a bit. These guys are really isolated and my life stories bring him back. He thinks they are kind of funny; in a cute way I can tell he gets a kick out of it."—Julie

You need to be supportive.

"My boyfriend goes through so many physical tests, mental tests, and challenges of character on a semiregular basis. And the moving around and traveling thing can make him pretty lonely at times. For some guys this is hard to admit, especially because they think they are supposed to be strong and so they feel stupid for feeling lonely. Let him know you are there for him, and send him little packages so that he doesn't feel so alone. Oh, and you can't be paranoid. Since you're not around him all the time you can't really see who he's hanging out with. Couple that with an active imagination and you could drive yourself crazy."—Jenny

Make plans to visit him.

"Now that we can afford it, we'll buy airline tickets and meet at hotels or bed-and-breakfasts in random places for the weekend, like San Diego, Chicago, Kansas City. It's been a nice way to experience something only we share together. Plus, he can get time off to see you. In fact, my boyfriend gets more time off than I do! It works the same way vacation time at a 'normal' job does. Whenever he goes to training on other bases, he's not really supposed to go out of the state. Anytime they leave the base during training, they have to sign in and out, and if they're going out of the state, they need to give the base contact information and the exact destination where they can be reached. As long as he has a cool supervisor, it's not usually a problem."—Carey

Talking Shop

Here's a list of key words and phrases that will help you speak his language:

Absolute dud: No, this has nothing to do with the guy you are dating. An absolute dud is a nuclear weapon that fails to explode when it's launched at a target.

Acoustic jamming: No, we're not referring to those weekly jam sessions with his musically inclined buddies. Acoustic jamming is the deliberate radiation of the enemy's mechanical signals.

Chicks: Relax, he's not talking about the women at the military base. Chicks are friendly fighter aircraft.

Gap: Not to be confused with the place he buys his cargo pants. A gap is an area within a minefield that is free of live mines and obstacles.

Lay leader: This has nothing to do with getting laid. A lay leader is a volunteer appointed to meet the needs of a particular religious faith group when their military chaplains are not available.

Dummy run: Any simulated firing practice. Also called a *dry run*.

Escort: If your boyfriend tells you he's acting as an escort, chances are he's not talking about being an escort for women. An escort refers to a unit assigned to accompany and protect another force or convoy.

Reserve: Members of the military services who are not in active service but who are subject to call to active duty. It's usually easier to date a guy in the reserves than it is to date a guy on active duty.

Engagement: Don't go shopping for rings just yet. An engagement has nothing to do with the status of your relationship. An engagement refers to a tactical conflict.

chapter 15 The Airline Pilot

He's that charming, distinguished-looking guy sitting on the left side of the airplane in the cockpit, complete with his uniform. And just as you settle into your seat and get ready to relax, you hear his deep, soothing voice come on the sound system to welcome you aboard. He makes a cute joke, some sort of gesture to connect with his passengers, and immediately you feel safe. We're going to be fine, you think to yourself. He's a good pilot. And when you touch down and get ready to leave the plane, there he is again, standing at the door of the airplane and wishing you a pleasant stay. He has a strong presence. And although you would never stop and ask him for his number (he looks too professional in that uniform), you can't help but wonder where he's heading. After all, what could be sexier than dating an airline pilot?

His Look

Neat, professional, distinguished. Pilots have a masculine presence when they're in uniform. Take them out of their work clothes and they look a bit out of place. Note: This guy has no personal sense of style. His regular clothes are all casual and a bit dorky.

His Vibe

He's romantic, smooth, adventurous, and rumor has it, not always that faithful when it comes to women. This guy has a reputation for being a jet-setting ladies' man who takes off his wedding ring at the airport, leaving a trail of broken hearts across the country. Pilots are known to be confident, outgoing, romantic, and a touch arrogant. Note: It's not uncommon for a pilot to hit on an attractive flight attendant.

His Hours

Hours depend solely on seniority. New pilots fly reserve, which means they have no set flying schedule. Instead they are placed on call for two or three weeks at a time, just waiting to be called at any minute to fill in for a pilot who is ill. Those on reserve have to be packed up and ready to fly at any given moment. More senior airline pilots have a regular flight schedule, with no more than 8 hours of flying time on a domestic flight and 16 hours on an international flight. Note: By law pilots cannot fly more than 100 hours per month and no more than 1,000 hours per year.

Risk Factor

Constant travel, lack of communication (you can't get ahold of him when he's in the air), plus you never really know where this guy is or what he's doing during all that downtime. Pilots have a reputation for cheating, and it's incredibly easy for them to do it. When the crew has late-night flights away from home base, they travel together to a nearby hotel, where they often spend evenings together eating dinner or exploring the city.

Perks

He's romantic and attentive, at least when he's with you. The constant travel, though difficult at times, can also make your relationship spontaneous and exciting. When he's with you, it's for such a short period of time that he'll most definitely be on his best behavior. Pilots pride themselves on taking care of the women they date (even if they're dating more than one woman at a time). And if he's staying somewhere romantic for more than one night, chances are you can fly out with him (for little money) for a romantic getaway. Note: On average he'll make close to $110,000 a year. Salaries depend on the type of aircraft they are flying, the number of miles and hours they have flown, and whether or not they work for a major airline. Plus, airline pilots fly free and they get great hotel deals across the country.

What Kind of Frequent Flyer Is He?

- **The commercial airline pilot:** Most of these guys spend their days transporting passengers and cargo from one destination to another, although a small number of them are involved in aircraft testing and flight instruction. Those who work for major airlines, transporting passengers, can most likely be found in one of two positions: the pilot (also known as the captain) and the copilot (also called the first officer).
- **The private jet pilot:** This guy has one of the sexiest jobs around. Most likely he's been trained as a commercial airline pilot but then landed (no pun intended) the highly coveted gig of transporting the rich and famous. Expect this guy to fly to exotic locations for days at a time (on occasion he might be able to take you with him), transporting some of the wealthiest people in the world.
- **The helicopter pilot:** These pilots could work for private businesses or government bodies. Duties might include monitoring traffic (for local news stations), search and rescue operations, emergency medical transportation, law enforcement, and newsgathering.

Will You Rule Him Out?

Before you decide, here's a look at what to expect when you are dating an airline pilot.

Rule #1:
Everything about his job is based on seniority.

A pilot's position, what salary he makes, what plane he flies, and what schedule he has are based solely on how many years he's been with the airline. Those who are just starting out will have unpredictable hours; chances are they'll be on reserve, which means they won't know when they'll be called out to fly a plane. In addition, the more junior he is, the worse his flight times are going to be. Note: If he's on call and he gets paged, there's nothing he can do about it, even if he's in the middle of your birthday dinner. As for the more senior guys, they have a set flight schedule. Still, pilots are constantly traveling, which makes for quite a lonely existence, especially for the person he leaves behind.

Rule #2:
Just because he's attentive and romantic doesn't mean he's faithful.

Pilots are known to be romantic, spontaneous, and incredibly attentive to the women they date. And why wouldn't they be? They have plenty of downtime and tons of space when they're out of town, which is quite often. So while your romantic jet setter might very well call you at every one of his stops (more than any banker or lawyer you've ever known) and send you sweet love e-mails when he's passing time in the pilot's lounge, don't be fooled. He could still make time for a nightcap with a willing flight attendant. So what should you do? "Does he call you in every city or just when he touches down in yours? Have you met his friends? Have you been to his house? Make sure you know what his life is like before you get too invested. Pilots can get involved with you without revealing too much about their own lives. And every time things get intense, he can take off for a few months. This could be the perfect scenario for a guy. Just make sure you don't get stuck in it," says Jamie.

Rule #3:
He will bond with flight attendants and other crew members during layovers.

Expect your guy to stay in the same hotel, and sometimes on the same floor, as the rest of his crew, including the flight attendants. Airline pilots and crew members have a significant amount of downtime during layovers, especially on international flights, so it's not uncommon for the team to get together in the evening for drinks, dinner, or some nearby sightseeing. Drinking, eating, and shopping together are the most typical ways to pass the time, though drinking is the most popular—and more often than not, it's the pilots who encourage this sort of camaraderie. It is unlikely that these people have ever worked together before and so it is always an interesting dynamic when the crew gets together to socialize. Note: Those who go straight to their hotel room and shut the door, rather than going out drinking with everyone else, are usually called *slam-clickers*.

Rule #4:
It's hard to keep a new relationship going when he's always away.

Between the flight times that make him inaccessible for hours on end to the different time zones that make it almost impossible to connect, this is one of the hardest relationships to keep going. Still, if he loves you and he wants this to work, he will make the extra effort. "He started to send me text messages when we were in different time zones," says Heather. "It was just an easy way to let me know that he arrived safely and that he missed me. At first I loved hearing from him that way, but then I noticed that he was sending me text messages more often than he was calling, and with all the rumors about pilots being players, I started to worry. It turned out that I was right. He was seeing other people, not seriously, but enough that we were getting nowhere. The thing is I don't even blame him for it. In the beginning of a pilot's career, there's no structure to his schedule and no way to plan your lives together. We would go out on two or three great dates at a time and then he'd leave for two weeks. Since it was the beginning of our relationship, it was almost impossible to get into a groove."

Rule #5:
Pilots are adventurous and romantic.

Most airline pilots have wanted to have their jobs since they were little boys. Perhaps it was their desire to see the world that got them excited or maybe they just loved the idea of flying a powerful jet. Whatever the case may be, this guy couldn't survive anywhere else, especially at a nine-to-five desk job. Airline pilots are far from boring. In fact, these guys are some of the most adventurous, spontaneous men out there, so get ready for the ride of your life. "He was the most exciting boyfriend I've ever had," says Pauline, "and all the travel and the saying goodbye and missing each other all the time made things more romantic and intense. He'd be on call for three weeks at a time and without any notice he'd get called to fly to Europe for a week. And then some weeks he'd be completely off and we could just spend time together. He used to fly private jets, not commercial jets, so he would take some of the wealthiest people around the world, and twice I got to go with him! It was amazing and incredibly romantic. Plus, watching your boyfriend fly a plane is a major turn on."

Rule #6:
When he's not working he will be completely focused on you.

Unlike the rest of the world, pilots don't think about work once they leave the airport. Though he might have several days of travel ahead of him, he will also have several days off to relax. And when pilots are not scheduled to fly, they can live a completely uninterrupted existence. What does this mean for you? When he's with you, he's really with you. That means no multitasking, no networking, and no late-night status calls.

He Says . . .

We need someone who's independent.

"We chose a life of travel, which is not easy for most women to grasp, but it suits us. And the reality is that the more senior our position is with the airline, the better our schedule is and the easier it is to coordinate our plans in advance. Still, we understand how hard it is to keep saying goodbye to us and to have us away sometimes one or two weeks at time. That's why it's so important for a pilot to date someone who's either superbusy and career-focused, or extremely independent. She also needs to be trusting. Remember, we spend the majority of our time in the cockpit."—Dave

She Says . . .

Get ready for the ride of your life.

"He was by far the most romantic, attentive guy I've ever been with. Pilots pride themselves on being able to make women happy and so these guys are always sending flowers, making special plans for when you see each other, calling when they arrive in different cities to tell you they miss you. Most of them are pretty adventurous, too. My ex-boyfriend was always going skydiving and rock climbing. We ended up breaking up after college because our lifestyles were just so different. Once I started working in the corporate world, I couldn't enjoy all those perks, like flying to Europe to meet him on a layover, so things just sort of fizzled out."—Paula

Talking Shop

Here's a list of key words and phrases that will help you speak his language:

A & P technicians: No, these guys don't provide technical support for the supermarket! A&P stands for "airframe and power plant" (not that this clarifies anything). All you need to know is that these guys are licensed by the FAA to keep aircraft in safe flying condition.

Blackout: This has nothing to do with a power outage, though it may be just as frustrating. A blackout is the seasonal period (usually around the holidays) when special fares and employee discounts are not available.

Buddy pass: Yippee! A perk for you! Though you might not want to be referred to as his buddy, this pass, if given to you by an employee, allows you to fly on a discounted travel ticket.

Cattle call: This sounds more degrading than it is. A cattle call is a group interview process used to hire flight attendants.

Deadhead: No, we are not talking about Jerry Garcia fans. A deadhead is a crew member flying as a passenger to reach an assignment in another location. Who would have thought that having a *deadhead* on the airplane would actually make you feel safer?

Federal Aviation Administration (FAA): The government agency responsible for air safety and operation of the air traffic control system. The FAA also administers a program that provides grants from the Airport and Airway Trust Fund for airport development.

Layover: An overnight stay for a flight crew member in a city other than his home base. It is not unlikely for a pilot to have a series of layovers. Most likely other crew members, including the flight attendants and copilots, will have the same layover and stay in the same hotel.

Plucker: A terrible name for the flight attendant who collects your ticket at the gate.

Per diem: A regulated daily allowance for crew members to spend while they are away from their home base. Though it's not a huge chunk of cash, it's nice pocket change for the two of you—that is, if you decide to join him on one of his layovers.

Flight plan: A required planning document that covers the expected operational details of a flight such as destination, route, fuel on board, etc. It is filed with the appropriate FAA air traffic control facility. Note: If you think your pilot boyfriend is lying about his route, casually check out his flight plan.

Flight release: Yes, even pilots have paperwork! The flight release is the paperwork that the captain (also known as the pilot) signs stating that the crew is fit for the flight.

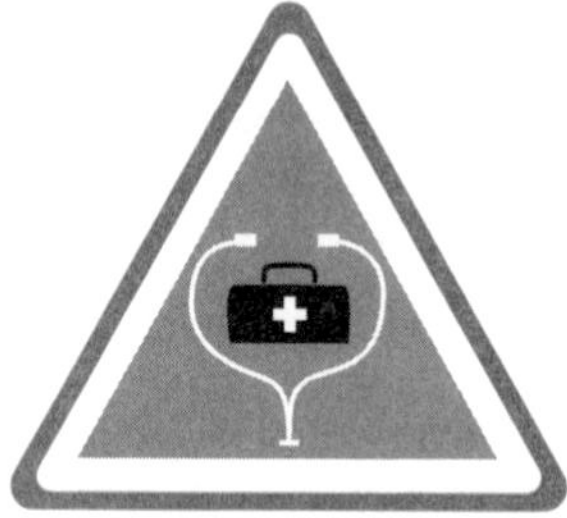

part 5: The Doctors

You're dating a doctor. Hooray! Your mother will be so pleased. And he's actually quite charming, once he loosens up a bit. After all, what's not charming about dating a guy who saves other people's lives? He takes you for drinks on the first two dates, then eventually decides you are dinner worthy. And when he walks you home from dinner (of course he walks you home; doctors are good guys), he checks your tonsils for inflammation and teaches you how to give proper mouth-to-mouth. By week three, you've tried on his white coat and touched his stethoscope; you even wear a pair of his surgical pants to bed at night. His patients call him Doctor; you call him your very own Patrick Dempsey. Things are great. You're dating a doctor—and dying to play on his examination table. But, what's this about being at the hospital on the night of your birthday? That's right, eager beaver, just when things seemed perfect, the love doctor lays it all out on the table: his "on call" schedule. Being "on call" is a tradition in the medical field. It means that your man has to stay in the hospital overnight. What does this mean for you? Your significant other or soon-to-be could be working up to thirty-six hours with little or no sleep. Not just once, either. This occurs every second, third, or fourth night depending on the institution and the specialty he is in. While this could be the perfect girls' night out or in, it can also be a major drag because it is immediately followed by postcall. And, if there's anything worse than being on call, it's being postcall. This is the twenty-four-hour time period after one is on call. True, you get to be near him, but you should expect him to display the following symptoms: acne, exhaustion, bed head, disinterest in anything you say, memory loss, and lack of sex drive. So, what's it really like to date a doctor? Though it can be frustrating because at times you'll barely see him, it really depends on what stage of his career he's in and the specialty he chooses. Before you take a stab at it, here's a look at what you might be getting into.

the lowdown

his job	personality traits	most commonly used gadget	how he spends his weekends	his biggest concern
resident	confident, detailed, anal	surgical gloves	on call	not killing anyone
psychiatrist	patient, attentive, self-assured	the couch	relaxing, reading up on new psychological disorders	having a patient commit suicide

chapter 16

The Resident

He's that adorable guy walking down the street in his white lab coat and green surgical pants, with his hospital ID tag hanging from his front pocket. And even before you see his face, you find yourself intrigued. I mean, what's more attractive than a guy who spends his days learning how to save lives? You stop next to him and wait for the streetlight to change, but you can't seem to get up the nerve to talk to him. Why? He seems so focused and purposeful, plus he's completely unaware of your presence. You try to formulate an introduction, but for the first time in a while you feel intimidated. After all, this guy really saves people, so what would he want with you? But just as you begin to conquer your inferiority complex, the streetlight turns green and Mr. Fantasy

Guy checks his pager, then walks quickly back to the hospital. So, is dating a doctor really as dreamy as you think?

His Look

Clean-cut, neat, and relatively pale. Most likely this guy hasn't had a vacation in ages and chances are he hasn't been shopping in ages either. When he's working at the hospital expect him to wear his white lab coat with either scrubs (surgical pants) or a suit and tie (depending on hospital policy). The remainder of his wardrobe consists of mostly basics: slacks, suits, jeans, sweatshirts, and button-downs. This guy is far from stylish, and he has no clue about fashion trends. Most likely he still thinks it's the 1990s, which was the last time he paid attention to what was "in." This is not his fault. He has no time to keep up with the trends.

His Vibe

Focused, intense, and a bit socially uncomfortable. He's spent so much time in the hospital around sick people that he'll have trouble adjusting to the outside world. Remember, he's had no practice schmoozing at the "office." So, while most guys had to strengthen their social skills in order to pitch clients and sign deals, this guy was busy studying cadavers. He's also under a tremendous amount of pressure and may secretly fear that he will kill someone on the job or make a mistake that will get him sued. So how do you get this guy to unwind a little? Talk about your ailments, show him your scars, discuss past surgery, family illness, etc. Chances are he'll lighten up and feel right at home.

Risk Factor

He may have a huge ego. Most doctors have a bit of a God complex, and therefore feel pardoned from any painful family holiday or dreaded errand. Also, expect him to suffer from constant exhaustion and a lack of sex drive. He's overworked and underpaid, and chances are he won't make any substantial money until he's thirty-five. He also can't commit to any plans with you until he gets his on-call schedule at the first of every month. Oh, and doctors make the worst patients. When they have a cold they act like they're dying. Your biggest threat: Nurses (in the hospital) and drug reps that stalk him at the office and take him out to lunch.

Perks

He has a very honorable career. He's also motivated, intelligent, honest, dedicated, and incredibly organized. Plus, he's a doctor now, which means that he can prescribe medicine! Expect drug samples (everything from birth control pills to allergy medicine) and plenty of drug paraphernalia (you'll have a plethora of Viagra pens and Prozac mouse pads). Oh, and with those license plates, you'll always get good parking! Note: Eventually he will make a very nice, stable living.

Will You Rule Him Out?

Before you decide, here's a look at what to expect when you're dating a resident.

Rule #1:

This guy doesn't have the time to play games.

If he likes you, he will call. Residents don't have the finances, the time, or the energy to play games. In fact, they are a bit clueless on how to intrigue women. They are far from smooth, they don't know much about what's going on in the outside world, and chances are they won't understand what you do for a living unless it's in health care or social work. So, if he's not a game player, what are the risks of dating a doctor? Your biggest initial challenge will be getting him to fall for you. Doctors have so little free time that unless they are floored by you immediately, chances are they won't start a relationship. Why? It takes time to build a relationship and they just don't have any. Plus, they are easily distracted by work and therefore less likely to spend their workday daydreaming about your future together.

Rule #2:

He's terrible at flirting.

Doctors spend so much time in the hospital around sick people that he won't have the time to develop a postcollege personality. Expect your first date to feel more like an interview rather than a courting period. Doctors are very time-efficient. Chances are he's blocked out an hour in his schedule to meet you and decide, right then and there, if you're actually worth his free time. "Though it's not easy to admit, I went on a blind date with a doctor that lasted no more than ten minutes. He met me at a coffee shop in the middle of a snow storm and he must have decided on the spot that I wasn't right for him," says Danielle. "When he ordered my coffee, he asked for it in a to-go cup. I don't think he was trying to be mean; I just think he didn't have time to waste. I can't say that it wasn't a little hard on my ego, but in a way I guess it was sort of refreshing."

Rule #3:
He's not great at small talk.

Remember, doctors are used to dealing with patients all day, which means that they don't have experience having to win over a client, present an ad campaign, or lunch with the boss. Translation? He's not very smooth. He's also not very knowledgeable as far as what's going on in the rest of the world, which limits his ability to chitchat. So, don't expect him to know the latest news (he doesn't have time to read the newspaper) or anything about the TV shows you watch, or the new Seven jeans you are wearing. Leah, an editor for a women's magazine says, "I used to think that my boyfriend just wasn't interested in that stuff, but one day I caught him sitting in my living room, mesmerized by an issue of *People* magazine. He picked it up from my coffee table and he was completely hooked. That's when I realized it wasn't so much that he didn't like that silly stuff, it was just that he never had the time to get into it. You have to be patient with these guys. Teach them how to relax and be silly. In a way, you have to reintroduce them to life because the reality is that they've missed a lot of it."

Rule #4:
All doctors, even the nice, thoughtful ones, secretly feel that they are the greatest contribution to society.

Don't take it personally when his eyes glaze over the minute you start to talk about your job, because most likely he doesn't understand what you do for a living and sadly, he will have trouble sympathizing with what you believe to be a stressful day. "It's amazing that doctors go through all this training and yet they truly can't grasp the idea of public relations," says Jessica. "It took my ex-boyfriend two years to take any interest in my job. And even then, I could tell that he didn't really understand the point of it. Put a doctor in a room with a bunch of bankers and consultants and he's lost. Introduce him to the one doctor in the room (providing that this guy is not a dentist), and he's in heaven. It's like they have their own little club and no one else really gets it except for them. I've come to terms with it, but it can be frustrating at times."

Rule #5:
He won't be able to change his call schedule, unless it's an emergency.

All residents have an on-call schedule and though they may be able to swap a date or two with another resident well in advance, it's not something they should be expected to do often. The good news is that unlike lawyers and investment bankers, residents know their schedules a month ahead of time and they are great planners. As a result, he shouldn't have to cancel plans with you at the last minute.

Rule #6:
Don't expect him to send you cute e-mails during the day.

Remember, this guy is not sitting at his desk all day. Most likely he won't have an office line nor will he be on his computer checking e-mails, sending you love notes, or shooting off the occasional instant message. Do yourself a favor and don't expect to hear from him during the day. He is surrounded by sick people all day long, which leaves him little time to think about you. Remember, one hour for you, sitting in front of your computer, feels like five minutes to him. Don't be surprised if you don't hear from him all day. "I used to hate that we couldn't talk during the day, especially when something bad happened at the office," says Jennifer. "I remember wanting to call my boyfriend just to vent. I'd try him at the hospital but when I would finally get ahold of him he'd answer the phone with that rushed voice. He'd say, 'What's up?' in that way that makes you know that he's not available. And so I'd let it go. But by the time he'd come home that night all the drama would be kind of over. And even if I still wanted to talk about it, he'd be so tired that he wouldn't be able to listen to my story and give good advice."

Rule #7:
Doctors talk about things that are not comfortable to normal people.

This guy has lost his ability to determine what is and what is not appropriate. Don't be surprised if he talks to your boss in detail about an open-heart surgery he witnessed or a patient who has yellow leathery skin due to jaundice. "I once dated a guy," says Leah, "who showed me pictures he'd developed from a wedding we went to and as part of the roll of film, he had five or six pictures of himself with his cadaver. To him it was no big deal. He was like, 'Oh there we are in front of the chuppah, and oh the next one, that's just my cadaver . . . oh and here we are on the dance floor.' It was gross!"

He Says . . .

Try to be patient with us.

"We know that dating a doctor can be a pain in the butt. Trust us, we wish we had more time with you and even with our friends. But you have to realize that it will not always be like this; if it were, we would never make it through. We're all working toward something. And if you're the person we're supposed to be with, then we should be working toward it together."—Eric

We need to be with a woman who is independent and busy.

"My last girlfriend was a writer and maybe it's because she was home all day, but I felt like she was just sitting at home waiting for me to come home. It was like this incredible pressure to entertain her when I got home at night, and I remember dreading it because I was exhausted. Now I have an amazing girlfriend and it's not like she's in the health care field or anything. She's just independent and busy, and she has plans at night, too, so it works out great. She also respects that I chose to be a doctor and she understands all that goes into it."—Danny

Even we don't know exactly what we're getting into.

"Yes, we know we want to become doctors, but we have no real clue what that process entails. In the beginning I didn't even understand what it meant to be on call. I used to think that it meant that you could go home and go to sleep but that if you were paged you would have to go to the hospital. Now, of course, I know that it means you have to stay at the hospital overnight!"—Shawn

She Says . . .

Become friends with other doctors' girlfriends.

"Make sure that you become friends with other women who are dating or married to doctors. That's the best advice I can give. You need to be surrounded by people who understand what your life is like. Your friends might listen and be sympathetic, and they might think they understand, but they can't fully understand. You need a support system. Oh, and if at all possible, date these guys after they finish medical school."—Julie

This guy doesn't like to spend a lot of money.

"Don't expect him to take you to fancy restaurants or have tickets to see anything. Dating a doctor is the opposite of dating a trader. This guy is not connected, he doesn't get work perks, and unless he has family money he's not raking in the cash, at least not for those first few years. "—Stacey

Don't put down the importance of your own work.

"In the beginning it was very hard for me. I am in advertising and while I am figuring out the best way to reach our target audience, my boyfriend is out there saving lives. It's easy to start thinking about how pointless your career is in comparison to theirs, but don't do it. And make sure that your guy doesn't make you feel like you are any less important either."—Nancy

He will be excused from every obligation.

"It gets to be frustrating when they finally have time to spend with you and they end up exhausted. My parents would excuse him from every family function because he was a doctor, and they thought that was just amazing, but I wasn't so easily swayed. One night Jason went with me to see my little sister in a school play and he fell asleep in the middle of it. I got so annoyed! And yet, there's really nothing you can do. I just wish we had met once his career was more established."—Stacey

Get used to going to events alone.

"He's not going to be around that much and chances are you are going to have to go to a lot of events and weddings by yourself. It's annoying after a while and the worst is that even when he's around and with you, he's not that fun because he's exhausted. My advice? Try to be as independent as possible and when you do start to fight, remind yourself that dating a doctor is a very difficult thing to do. Of course you are going to fight, because they are practically half asleep throughout your entire relationship. Just remind yourself why you are sticking it out with him. Hopefully he's worth it!"—Jodi

The Breakdown

Here's what you should know about the resident:

biggest turn on	He's smart and ambitious, plus he's saving lives
biggest challenge	Getting him to relax and unwind
best way to get in touch	Cell phone or pager
greatest perk	Your mother will love him
best timing	When he's done with his first year of residency

What Kind of Doctor Will He Be?

- **The Psychiatrist:** This guy is a bit socially uncomfortable, which seems odd considering it is his job to help others with their problems. No, he won't be analyzing you. Psychiatrists are often just as screwed up as the rest of us. The good news is that you'll seem normal next to the people he treats. The bad news is that when he's not working, he's relatively drained from hearing everyone else's problems.
- **The Pediatrician:** Sweet, caring, and somewhat simple. His days are relatively predictable and filled with crying babies who are sick with your basic colds and stomach flu. This guy will make a great father. Watching him with his patients will make you melt.
- **The Gynecologist:** Finally a guy who understands what women go through! He helps them with everything from pregnancy to pelvic exams and cancer prevention. Though this is a major advantage, the truth is that he has one of the most strenuous specialties with long hours and an unpredictable schedule. He could be called to the hospital at any hour, which means canceled trips, parties, dates, etc. Note: His patients are women, so he'll see lots of breasts and vaginas. No, he isn't turned on by this!
- **The Surgeon:** This guy is confident, cocky, and proud. And he should be. Surgery is one of the most demanding and competitive fields. Expect your guy to be meticulous, exacting, efficient, and well put together. He will save lives, change lives, and make a fortune while he's doing it. Expect him to be anal with everything—his shirts, ties, nails, etc. He has to be. Note: He has long, unpredictable hours. His life is not his own. As for the plastic surgeon, yes, he will touch and improve breasts, thighs, butts. That doesn't mean that he doesn't like the real thing.

Talking Shop

Here's a list of key words and phrases that will help you speak his language:

Cadaver: A dead body donated for medical research. Expect first-year medical students to name their cadaver and refer to him or her as if it's an actual person. Don't be alarmed, your guy's not crazy—everybody does this.

Chief resident: A doctor in his senior year of residency who assumes responsibility for overseeing interns and junior residents. The chief resident is selected by the attendings, and the title is considered a prestigious honor.

Fellowship: The period of training once you've completed your residency. A fellow falls somewhere between residents and faculty in the hierarchy. They are paid like advanced residents, but earn nothing close to what a private physician makes. Doing a fellowship looks great on his resume.

Internship: The first year of residency. An intern is an MD who is continuing to study in the hospital after graduating from med school. This guy can write prescriptions, but he's licensed to practice medicine only within the hospital.

The match: When residency applicants are accepted into residency programs. After applying to various programs in their chosen specialty, students submit a "rank order list," which specifies their preferences. Residency programs submit similar lists. This operates kind of like rushing a sorority house. After all of the lists have been received, a computer matches applicants and programs. At noon Eastern time on a specific day in March of each year, all applicants across the country receive an envelope telling them where they will spend the next several years. Get ready to pick up and move. It's quite possible that your guy might be matched in another city, which means he's going to pick up and move.

Moonlighting: No, we're not talking about Bruce Willis's hit TV show. If a doctor is moonlighting, he's working a second job at night. Doctors typically moonlight for another hospital. It's a great way to make extra money.

On-call schedule: His schedule of the nights he will be on call at the hospital. He gets his schedule the first of every month. Before that he has no idea which nights he'll be free.

Prognosis: Prediction of the probable course of a disease and the chances of recovery. Residents constantly give a prognosis for various patients.

Registered nurse (RN): Your competition. This person will work closely with your guy. She is someone who has attended nursing school, typically for four years, and received a degree in nursing. Registered nurses provide care to patients based on orders written by doctors.

Residency: Training in a specialty after graduating from medical school. This could last from three to seven years. Least demanding residencies: radiology, anesthesiology, and physical medicine and rehabilitation. Most demanding residencies: surgical interns and internal medicine interns.

chapter 17

The Psychiatrist

He's that seemingly calm guy sitting at the bar with all of his friends, watching them make fools of themselves as they unsuccessfully hit on various women. He's cute, in an unassuming way, and you can tell that even though he's not participating in his friends' childish escapades, he is getting a kick out of watching them. So, why isn't he the one up on the tables pledging his love to the waitress? Because he's more reserved than that. In fact, this guy is a bit more of an observer, so if you want to get to know him, chances are you're going to have to make the first move.

His Look

Far from eccentric, impulsive, or extravagant. This guy has a kind, conservative, traditional demeanor. Expect him to look professional; most likely he'll wear a dark suit and tie (even when he's at the hospital). Note: Some patients get so accustomed to how their therapist looks that they get nervous when he drastically changes his hairstyle.

His Vibe

Responsible, practical, calm, serious, and self-assured. This guy is not going to stand out in a crowd, nor is he going to make an impulsive decision (like a Wall Street trader). The psychiatrist is used to being a constant for his patients. He's not an attention seeker, nor is he a wild party guy. If anything, this guy is more of an attentive observer. Remember, his job is to listen to other people and to allow them to focus on their own issues.

Risk Factor

He's egotistical and he'll have trouble admitting when he's wrong. Some psychiatrists think they are untouchable and immune from any of the issues and problems their patients might have. Plus, this guy is so used to discussing his patients' problems that he will eventually forget to focus on his own.

Perks

Yes, he will let you talk about your problems (more than most guys), and the majority of the time he will listen and provide feedback. Psychiatrists are generally kindhearted, even-keeled individuals who like helping people. And as if that's not good enough, these guys make their own schedules. What does this mean for you? He won't work late nights or have to travel on business trips.

The Breakdown

Here's an analysis of the psychiatrist:

biggest turn on	He understands the human mind
biggest challenge	Getting him to admit when he's wrong
best way to get in touch	At his office, in between patients
greatest perk	He makes a living helping people; he's a good listener
best timing	When he has his own practice

Will You Rule Him Out?

Before you decide, here's a look at what to expect when you're dating a psychiatrist.

Rule #1:
Just because he's a therapist doesn't mean he's analyzing you.

No, he's not analyzing the way you eat, smile, part your hair, etc. Though you may not realize it, analysis takes a significant amount of time (which is why people in analysis see their doctors three to four times a week), and it's not like this guy has superhuman powers. There's no magic to psychiatry. It takes time, years of training, and plenty of focus to be able to understand a patient's patterns, issues, and inner conflicts. So, before you drive yourself crazy wondering what he thinks of you, try to relax. These guys tend to turn off that analytical side of them when they're outside of the office anyway.

Rule #2:
Psychiatrists have issues too; they just have a hard time admitting them.

He spends his days focusing on other people's issues and unless he's in therapy as well (which is always a bonus), there's a good chance he's started to ignore his own issues. This is not entirely his fault, but it's also not acceptable, especially if he has issues that bother you. Understand that he will have a hard time admitting his own faults. He may see his faults as personal failures. After all, he's supposed to be the expert on this stuff, right? Make sure he can take himself off that pedestal to join you in the real world.

Rule #3:
Don't be jealous of his patients.

Yes, he will spend most of his time sitting in a room (with people you don't know) listening to their most intimate problems. And you might be jealous of the fact that they have his undivided attention for a full hour, without any distractions, when you can barely get him to turn down the TV to listen to you. Still, try to remember that this is his line of work and that when he's with his patients, he's in a completely different mindset than when he's with you.

Rule #4:
He thinks he has the answers to everything.

He is used to being the expert. After all, people come to him every day for help on how to handle their lives, and they pay him! So, it's only natural that after a while he will begin to think he's some sort of all-knowing guru. Don't let him get away with this mentality, because it's far from true. Therapists do not have all the answers! Though they may have a good understanding of the human psyche, and they also may be very good at what they do in the office, they do not know everything, and they are certainly not exempt from taking responsibility in their own lives. Just think about it: Why do you think he went into this profession to begin with? Probably to understand his own issues!

Rule #5:
He will not be able to discuss his patient's problems with you.

This may be difficult to get used to, especially when he comes home drained, but it's important for you to understand. He is not keeping secrets; he's just keeping someone's confidence, and there's a big difference. Try not to pry too much; he may think you don't respect his work. Chances are if he wants to tell you a bit about a patient, he will find a way to work it into a discussion without revealing who he's talking about. Whatever you do, don't drill him about various female patients that he might see in the office!

Rule #6:

Building a private practice takes time.

Yes, these guys spent eight-plus years training for the moment they can open up their own practice, but that doesn't mean it's an easy thing to do. "This could be one of the most stressful times in his career," says Jenny. "My boyfriend was so used to having a set schedule. His life was all mapped out for him whether that meant going to class, being at the hospital, or studying for the boards. When he started his practice, he rented an office, set up his phone line and computer, and just kind of panicked. It was like, okay, now what? My advice is to give him a chance to settle in. Whatever you do, don't pressure him to have a full schedule of patients right away. This will happen. After all, you don't become a doctor if you're lazy. These are some of the most dedicated, persistent people and they are not known to be impulsive or irrational, so they won't handle their practice that way either. It took my boyfriend two months to get his first patient and now, one year later, he has a pretty full schedule."

He Says . . .

At times it can be emotionally draining.

"I might see a schizophrenic patient in the morning, followed by a severely depressed woman who can barely function. Yes, we love what we do, but that doesn't mean it doesn't affect us at times. Occasionally I just need to relax a bit after work . . . just watch some sports, zone out, and feel normal."—Mike

We are not analyzing you, we promise.

"If anything, we might even be less aware of your quirks because we are just enjoying your company. So many women I've dated think that I am sizing them up and categorizing them according to what syndrome they have. The truth is that it takes time to analyze a person; that's why analysis is such an intensive process (usually four times a week). I can't speak for every psychiatrist out there, but when I am not with a patient I am in a completely different mindset."—Seth

Don't be jealous.

"One of my girlfriends used to ask me if I had any attractive patients in my office. She wanted to know if they had crushes on me and whether they talked about their sex lives or started crying in my office. I think it made her feel uncomfortable that I was working one-on-one with female patients and talking with them about things they don't talk about with anyone else. My girlfriend was afraid that I knew my patients better than I knew her but you can't even compare the two; it's a completely different relationship. Plus we are in total work mode when we are in the office. It's just not the same."—Jeffrey

Success takes time.

"Don't pressure him when he's just starting out. I remember when I first started my practice. I rented an office and used my desk from high school. I set up two chairs, put my diplomas on the wall and just waited. I think I had two patients a week for the first six months, but gradually my practice started to build. Now I see an average of seven patients a day and I literally have to refer people because I am too busy. He will be successful. Just give him a chance." —Norm

She Says . . .

He's relatively isolated during the day.

"The good news is that he's not hanging out in the office working late nights with female coworkers. In fact, unless he has a secretary, which most of these guys don't need, or a female officemate, you have nothing to worry about. My boyfriend was one of the most honest, decent men I ever met! I never worried whether he would stray. In fact, he was probably one of the most consistent, predictable guys I've dated."—Sherri

He's still a guy.

"Just don't think that he's going to be this incredibly attentive guy who will spend hours discussing your needs without addressing his own. He's still a guy and he's still going to do things that annoy you, like never take the garbage out. If anything, look at it as refreshing. You wouldn't want someone that talked to you about every little problem you had. Trust me, eventually you'd find it annoying."—Kate

Talking Shop

Here's a list of key words and phrases that will help you speak his language:

Acting out: A common term psychiatrists use to describe a person's actions when they're faced with emotional conflict. "Acting out" may be harmful or, in controlled situations, therapeutic. Note: Don't allow him to use this phrase with you. Just because you're pissed at him about something doesn't mean you're "acting out." You're pissed. There's a difference and he should know that.

Catharsis: The therapeutic release of ideas through "talking out" conscious material. If your boyfriend doesn't feel like listening to your problems, tell him you think it would be extremely cathartic for you.

Defense mechanism: An automatic psychological process that protects you against anxiety. "Acting out" is a defense mechanism. So is compulsive behavior. Washing every countertop in your home as soon as you hear that your boyfriend can't come to a family dinner might be a defense mechanism.

Fantasy: Psychiatrists love this term! A fantasy is an imagined sequence of events that serves to express unconscious conflicts, to gratify unconscious wishes, or to prepare for anticipated future events. You might have a fantasy that your doctor boyfriend left his female patient in the waiting room so that he could be with you.

Free association: A technique used in psychoanalytic therapy (when the patient lies on the couch). The patient spontaneously says whatever comes to mind, revealing unconscious thoughts and feelings in the process. Just make sure your psychiatrist boyfriend doesn't free associate with you. Chances are he'll say something that he'll regret.

Transference: Another word that psychiatrists love to use. Transference is the unconscious assignment to others (usually the psychiatrist) of feelings and attitudes that were originally associated with important figures (parents, siblings, etc.) in one's early life. In other words, a patient might see her psychiatrist as a father figure and apply all of the feelings she has for her actual father onto her psychiatrist, whether those be feelings of love or hate.

part 6: The Athletes

He's strong, physically fit, and extremely competitive. And as you watch him from the sidelines you can't help but feel like a high school cheerleader all over again. After all, there's something so sexy about dating an athlete. Whether he's playing professional golf, football, or simply competing in a triathlon, chances are you won't be able to take your eyes off his body. Unfortunately he won't even take a second to notice yours. Athletes are some of the most focused people in the world, at least when they're in the middle of a game. So, don't expect him to take his eye off the ball for you, not even for a second. You wouldn't want to break his concentration, now would you?

the lowdown

his job	personality traits	most commonly used gadget	how he spends his weekends	his biggest concern
professional football player	driven, focused, strong	football	training, partying, watching sports	being drafted, not getting injured
golf pro	outgoing, encouraging, honest	golf club	playing golf	getting PGA certified
personal trainer	outgoing, aggressive	dumbbell	working out	his percentage of body fat

chapter 18 The Professional Football Player

He's that big, broad-shouldered guy with the soft eyes and the playful, mischievous smile. Most likely you've seen him training at the gym, playing golf with the guys, or out for celebratory drinks with his teammates. And even though everyone tells you not to get involved with a professional athlete, you can't help but find him irresistible. I mean, what could be so hard about dating a professional football player? Sadly, it's more difficult than you think. Though these guys are incredibly passionate, fun-loving men who get great perks and make tons of money, they're also under a tremendous amount of pressure to perform. Plus, the average life span of a football player's career is three and a half years, which means your celebrity athlete will have to live life as a regular guy sooner than you think. So, make sure you're falling in love with him and not his profession.

His Look

Strong, powerful, and confident. Unless he's the kicker or the quarterback, this guy's going to be pretty massive, so get used to his broad shoulders. Expect him to have huge muscles coupled with a boyish, mischievous grin, and an incredible tolerance for pain. As for his personal style, most likely he doesn't have one. Football players spend the majority of their time in uniform or workout gear. Dressing up means putting on a shirt he got free along with a comfortable pair of jeans and sneakers. This guy would much rather spend his money on cars, gadgets, women, and his house (or houses) than he would on a pair of new Prada loafers (who wants to see a big, burly football player in a pair of slides anyway?).

His Vibe

Confident, strong, and incredibly dedicated to the sport. These guys think they're invincible, and they never see the end of their careers coming. They work hard (they're driven and dedicated, and they truly love what they do) but they also play hard, so watch out! When this guy's not on the field, or training, he can be found "bonding" with his teammates at private parties in luxury suites, the backroom of a strip club, you name it. Professional athletes get treated like Hollywood celebrities, and that means first-class tickets, five-star hotels, female fans, free custom-made clothes (since so many of them don't fit into shirts off the rack), and pretty much anything their hearts desire. Plus, these guys can get away with almost anything.

His Hours

During football season, he's on the road frequently, which means that you'll rarely see him (though he should check in with you when he gets to the hotel) unless you join him on the road. Home games mean that you'll get to see him during the weekend, though you never know what kind of mood he'll be in. It all depends on how he played that day and whether his team won. During off-season, chances are you'll have plenty of time to see each other. His days will consist of three hours of training (don't be surprised if he expects you to time him while he does sprints at the local high school track), reading playbooks, and bonding with his teammates. He'll usually come home each day feeling exhausted. Note: The combine (a mass "job interview" for college football players who are hoping to get picked for the NFL draft) occurs in late February and the draft pick begins in mid-April. These are incredibly stressful times.

Risk Factor

Short-lived careers, serious injuries, peer pressure, female fans, and lots of travel. These guys are constantly on the road, and their motto is "what happens on the road stays on the road," so expect lots of partying and female fans. Groupies will wait outside his hotel, stalk him after the game, and throw their panties in his face. His career is pretty short-lived and unstable. An injury could end his career early, or he could be traded at any moment and expect you to pick up and join him.

Perks

He's passionate about what he does, which can be extremely exciting to be around. He's in phenomenal shape, every woman wants him, and you have him. When he's at the height of his game he'll get treated like a celebrity everywhere he goes, which means that when you're with him, you too will be treated that way. Expect free dinners, less waiting time at restaurants, free nights in five-star hotels, and constant upgrades. You'll get great seats to every one of his games, and you can't knock that VIP stadium parking. Note: Rookie football players make upwards of $190,000.

Playing Favorites?

Here's a look at a few of the NFL's most popular teams

- **Dallas Cowboys:** Known as "America's team" for their national support, these guys are the most revered by their fans. They've won five Super Bowls in eight visits. Well-known former players for the team include Emmitt Smith and Troy Aikman.
- **Green Bay Packers:** Known for their die-hard fans, who refer to themselves as Cheeseheads (yes, they actually wear yellow Styrofoam hats in the shape of cheese). Wisconsinites live and die for their football team. Their team has won twelve championships, more than any other team, and two of those were in 1966 and 1967, the first two Super Bowl championships ever played.
- **New England Patriots:** Referred to as "the dynasty," the Patriots have won three of the last four Super Bowl championships (2005, 2004, and 2002). These guys are the reason the salary cap was created (to even out the playing field). The Patriots are known for their teamwork and incredible coaching by Bill Belichick, as well as for the clutch performances of quarterback Tom Brady.

Will You Rule Him Out?

Before you decide, here's a look at what to expect when you are dating a professional football player.

Rule #1:

Female fans will throw themselves at him.

Female fans wait at the players' exit after the games. They'll stalk the hotel lobbies, come up to your guy in restaurants, nightclubs, you name it. In addition, these guys are away in different cities without their girlfriends, and surrounded by a bunch of their teammates who may or may not be single. Professional athletes like to party after games and it's not uncommon to find them drinking, flirting, and engaging in sexual activities with various women. Some girlfriends have come to accept this behavior, knowing that it's part of the culture. Others are in denial. "I dated a linebacker for two years and I would never do that again," says Lauren. "It's something you can do when you're young, but now I would never waste two years like that. I met him when I was reporting on a story and he was incredibly handsome and sweet, but in the end he cheated on me. It was such a crazy lifestyle. Women would go crazy at the sight of him. He had female fans throwing their underwear at his face when he would leave the field. There were women that would scream and cry when they saw him, like he was a rock star. One time he even had a stalker that made him a photo album with pictures of her! It was bizarre and scary. And in the end there were just too many long weeks on the road and I guess too much temptation."

Rule #2:
If you're his girlfriend, don't expect the other players' wives to acknowledge you.

Athlete's wives are some of the strongest, most independent women you'll find, but they're also cliquey and territorial. Maybe it comes from the fact that they had no idea what they were getting into when they married their football player husbands (the time away, the fear of adultery, etc.), but regardless, these women have a strong bond with one another. So what does this mean for you? Chances are you won't be welcomed into their club with open arms. Lauren says, "There's a huge difference between being a player's girlfriend and a player's wife. The wives are so used to new women coming in and out of these guys' lives that they're not about to jump in and get all chummy with you the minute your guy introduces you as his girl. In fact, don't be surprised if they barely acknowledge you. I was with my boyfriend for two years and the wives always treated me like I was his flavor of the week."

Rule # 3:
Athletes have a work hard, play hard mentality.

He's under a tremendous amount of pressure and there's always someone younger and more talented out there just waiting to be drafted. So, whether you're aware of it or not, your potential guy is constantly thinking about the game. When he's not on the field, he's practicing for the game, reviewing plays, or checking up on his competition—unless he's out partying with the guys. In that case he might be less focused on the sport and more focused on its fringe benefits.

At the height of his career, a football player will be treated like an A-list celebrity. He'll be surrounded by tons of money, women, liquor, and VIP access, which means no matter how grounded he once was (assuming you knew him before he went pro), he may eventually begin to lose perspective. These guys grow accustomed to having things handed to them at any given time. In the beginning of their careers it's all about the sport, but the more recognition they get, the more they realize what they are worth, and that's when things get tricky. "I met my boyfriend before he was drafted into the NFL and I noticed a big change once he realized that he was becoming a hot commodity. He started wanting better things and caring about things that he never thought about before. He used to be completely focused on the game, and at that point our biggest problem was that he was always training or practicing and he was never focused on me; he would train from 8 A.M. to 8 P.M. on weekends and then crash from exhaustion at night. But once he made pro, our problems changed. Soon he became focused on which car we had, how big the house was compared to the other guys on the team, etc. It's a very indulgent lifestyle, one that promotes a lot of crass, impulsive behavior," says Jessica. "I used to party with them a lot and we'd be hanging out with all the other players and their wives or stripper girlfriends. And there was so much flirting. The guys with stripper girlfriends would be checking me out and the ones with the wives and normal girlfriends would be checking out the strippers. It was like everyone wanted what they didn't have. Eventually I found out that my boyfriend was seeing a topless dancer. That's, of course, when I moved out. I heard that he married an Olympic speed skater. I think he ultimately needed someone with the same mentality and drive that he had."

Rule #4:
Not all professional football players are financially set for life.

Sure, these guys live the good life while they're on the field. They get treated like celebrities, they get free clothes, upgrades, and VIP treatment, but not every football player is making millions of dollars a year. In fact, rookie players make $190,000 a year, which is what a third-year law associate might make. Factor in that the pro ball player could get traded or injured at any moment, and you've got a pretty unpredictable career. According to the NFL Players Association, the average career span of a football player is about three and a half years, and the average salary is about $1.3 million. Sure, that's a nice chunk of change in a short period of time, but unless your guy knows how to invest it, it's not going to last a lifetime. "Careers are what doctors and lawyers have," says Joe, a former football player. "The NFL is just an opportunity to make a lot of money in a short period of time. But then what? Then you're left to figure it out on your own."

Rule #5:
He will choose the sport over you.

These guys are extremely dedicated and driven, and most of them have been working toward this moment since high school. Chances are they were the stars of their high school and college teams, and many of them have grown accustomed to having reporters and scouts attend their games to videotape, analyze, and evaluate their performance. So what does this mean for you? Football will always be his number one love, so expect him to miss family weddings and holidays to practice with the team. As for when he's playing a game, don't expect him to get off that field for any reason in the world, and that includes you going into labor or getting smashed in the face while watching the game from the sidelines. Take, for example, the incident where a well known hockey player's wife got hit by the hockey puck in the middle of his game. "She was bleeding like crazy," says Jenna, "and he just kept on playing while the EMS took her to the hospital. I remember I had this big argument about that with my boyfriend because he said he would do the same thing!"

Rule #6:
He will have a hard time transitioning into the real world after his football career is over.

Life after football can be an extremely difficult adjustment for men who have spent their entire lives pursuing the dream. Most of these guys were raised playing the game. It's their identity and their livelihood. And then one day it all ends. "It's pretty sad," says Jennifer. "These guys have been so focused on the game since high school that many of them never developed other skills, because they never thought about life beyond football. A lot of them end up severely depressed when they retire. The money stops rolling in, the VIP treatment stops, their agents who loved them and told them that they were

God no longer return calls. . . . It's a major shock. I've seen a few of my ex-boyfriend's friends go downhill, and the worst is when they live in the past, constantly talking about when they were on the field. They start drinking and blowing away their savings, and eventually they end up broke, and sometimes divorced." So what do the smart ones do? They make plans for after football. They pursue careers in real estate, finance, and of course, for most of them, sports. Lots of football players become sportscasters, radio commentators, coaches, etc.

Rule #7:
Don't expect him to compromise.

It's not that these guys don't care about your opinion, it's just that they are used to getting out their aggression on the field, so it's not as common for them to have to sit down and talk things through. Plus, when they come home from practice, they're physically exhausted, so the last thing they want to do is talk. "My boyfriend was under so much pressure to perform that he couldn't deal with any complaints I had, especially before the draft pick. He became completely detached a month before the draft, and then once he found out that he was the number one draft pick, he called to ask me to move in with him. It's kind of all or nothing with these guys. I packed up my stuff and moved in with him, but things didn't change. He still wasn't able to focus on me. He wanted me to live with him, but he didn't want me to talk about how difficult it was for me to adjust to a new city. We broke up a few months later," says Rachel.

The Breakdown

Here's the lowdown on the professional football player:

biggest turn on	Seeing him play the game that he loves
biggest challenge	The female fans, his travel schedule, the end of his career
best way to get in touch	Cell phone
greatest perk	Getting special treatment, free meals, and great service; being with someone who's so passionate about what he does
best timing	Off-season

He Says . . .

We can only focus on one thing at a time.

"We're incredibly focused when we're out there on the field. It's like you get into this zone where nothing else matters and it's all about the game, and that's the way it needs to be. It's this mentality that makes it hard for us to switch back into relationship mode. We're not multitaskers. We're not out on the field playing the game but also thinking about all the household things that we have to do or the fact that we need to pick up a birthday card for your mother on the way home. It doesn't work like that."—Jason

When we get home from training we're exhausted.

"Even though we're in good shape, we're still out there working our butt off, whether it's preseason practice or during the season. Yes, we'll be physically shot at times, especially after games that we've lost, and during those moments we just want to be left alone."—Carl

She Says . . .

A lot of athletes want to settle down early and get married.

"Maybe they want something stable in their lives or perhaps they've been working toward one goal for so long that all they are missing is a wife. Regardless of the reason, football players tend to get married early and a lot of them marry their high school sweethearts. That doesn't mean they're all faithful, but you have to admit, it's kind of odd that so many guys in their early twenties who are experiencing so much success already have wives and kids at home. Whatever the case may be, watch out. Just because he's ready to settle down doesn't mean that he's all grown up. We were the only couple that wasn't married or engaged out of all of his friends, and thank God! So many of them got married too early and you could tell that they weren't very happy. What's the rush?"—Carrie

It was just a matter of time before he cheated.

"I never really caught him cheating, but I knew it was happening. We had a long-distance relationship for a year, and near the end it started to get more difficult to see each other. First he started calling less. He would check into a hotel and not check in with me or go to bed without calling . . . things like that. Then the last time I visited him I found some sex toys in his closet that I had never seen before. He never admitted anything and I didn't press him on it too much because I suspected it already. At that point we had already drifted apart. You have to really want it to work and both people have to put in the effort."—Lauren

They're not as tough as they look.

"Although these guys appear very strong, confident, good-looking, and popular, they're actually pretty sensitive and needy. Their cocky "I don't need anybody" attitude is a total act. Every athlete I've ever dated has turned out to be sensitive. In fact, most of them want to be nurtured and taken care of."—Erica

Talking Shop

Here's a list of key words and phrases that will help you speak his language:

The combine: A mass "job interview" for college football players who hope to be selected in the NFL draft. This occurs months before the draft and could eliminate your guy from being eligible for the NFL. It's incredibly stressful and players are put through physical tests, medical examinations, and a slew of questions to make sure they're in physical and mental shape for pro football. Beyond their physical appearance (yes, even the size of their calves matters), these guys are examined by doctors who check them for possible arthritis, unstable joints, or old injuries that could be aggravated.

Draft pick: One of the most stressful and emotional moments of his life, and yours too if you are together at the time. This is the moment he has been working toward his whole life. And who knows, he could be moving across the country or living in the middle of nowhere, depending on which team picks him. The draft pick is the selecting of collegiate players for entrance into the National Football League. It's not uncommon to see a football player get emotional (even teary-eyed) after being drafted to a great team. Note: The team with the worst record in the NFL over the previous season is allowed to select the first player in the draft.

Fumble: If your guy fumbles the ball during a game it means that he drops the ball while it's still in play. If this happens to him, chances are he's going to be in a bad mood when the game is over. A fumble could make or break the entire game, and even if it doesn't, it's an embarrassing move.

Game clock: The scoreboard clock that shows the amount of playing time in each quarter of the game. These guys are constantly watching the clock and if you're a true sports fan, you will too.

Muff: Relax; it's not what you think! Though football players may have a bad reputation, when they are on the field they're all about business. So what's a muff? It's when a player touches a loose ball in an unsuccessful attempt to obtain possession.

Off-season: Most likely your favorite time of year. This is the period of the year after the final game is over and before training camp opens. Expect your guy to have plenty of time to spend with you.

Overtime: An extra period tacked onto the end of a game when regulation play ends in a tie. This is an incredibly crucial time, so if you've been zoning out during most of the game, now's the time to start paying attention. The outcome of the next few minutes of play will determine his mood and yours.

Playoffs: The postseason tournament that determines the NFL champion. To get into the playoffs, a team must either win its division or have one of the two best records of all nondivision winners in its conference. This can be an incredibly exciting time for both of you. It's huge if your guy's team gets into the playoffs, and even though he'll be extremely busy, the excitement will make it all worthwhile.

Preseason: Right after training camp (which is usually at the end of July). Preseason means exactly what you would think. It's the period of time before the regular season. This is when your guy starts playing exhibition games and begins to check out new players. Though this is not an incredibly stressful time, it is an adjustment for both of you. He will be gearing up for another football season, which means his priorities will readjust and he'll have less time for you. Preseason in the NFL usually lasts from the beginning of August through Labor Day, when the regular season starts. Note: Make plans for the second half of the summer!

Regular season: The actual football season, not including preseason or the playoffs. In the NFL, the regular season lasts for seventeen weeks (although it may seem longer to you), during which teams play sixteen games to determine their eligibility and ranking going into the playoffs.

Rookie: The term used to describe a player in his first season in the NFL. Just like any other newbie in any other industry, the rookie is often given the grunt work. Don't be surprised if your tough NFL boyfriend is forced to carry other people's bags or supply doughnuts for the veteran football players. It's just the way it goes.

Scouts: Talent agents who attend college games to videotape, analyze, and evaluate a player's performance with the hope of signing him. Note: All professional football players are represented by agents.

Super Bowl: The National Football League's championship game.

chapter 19

The Golf Professional

He's that one guy on the golf course without a cell phone holster attached to his belt. And although he might be playing eighteen holes with some of the most powerful men on Wall Street or Capitol Hill, he has no intention of doing business with them, let alone writing off his weekly Saturday morning foursome. Why? Because being on the golf course is part of his job, and beyond the day-to-day pleasures of teaching golf, running operations, and repairing clubs, this all-American country club golf pro is pretty damn happy with his life. That's right; he has no drama, no stress headaches, and no unexpected late nights at the office. So even though he might pick you up for your date wearing head-to-toe golf paraphernalia (these guys wear golf clothes all the time, regardless of whether or not they've just come from work), he'll be entirely focused on you. And when he does share his work with you, chances are he'll be smiling ear to ear recalling some story about a specific golf lesson he gave, a tremendous shot he made, or something funny that happened to one of his coworkers. The only drawback? He loves being on the golf course so much that sometimes he'd actually rather be at work than sitting at home with you.

His Look

Far from materialistic. This guy is all golf, all the time, and until Gucci comes out with golf clothes, he won't come close to wearing anything designer. This guy's closet is filled with pleated khaki pants, visors, and golf shirts. What does this mean for you? Your golf pro boyfriend is far from fashion forward. In fact, when it gets cold outside he'll think he's mixing things up by trading in his short-sleeve golf shirt for a long-sleeve one. Or if he feels really crazy, he'll test out his new windbreaker. And, as if that's not uniform enough, chances are he's sticking to one brand of golf clothes. Most golf pros get sponsored by specific companies, so they get free clothes sent to them all the time.

His Vibe

Outgoing, confident, and laid-back. Golf pros are incredibly encouraging and patient on the golf course. They have to be if they are teaching golf all day. This is not a job you get stuck in, so expect your guy to love life and to be content with what he does every day, from gripping clubs to giving lessons to managing tournaments. Plus, he's completely comfortable in his work environment. After all, he's the club pro, the head honcho, the big man on the course. Note: He's not financially driven.

His Hours

Despite the fact that he'll be working weekends (that's the bad part), his hours are pretty reasonable and predictable, unless he's studying for his professional certification exam. Other than that, his days might be longer before a big club tournament or right before the club opens for the season, but even then he'll be home in time for dinner.

Risk Factor

He won't make a ton of money, he has to work weekends, and women will hit on him when he's giving them private lessons. What does this mean for you? You won't be retiring anytime soon, unless he's a head pro, and even then it's a stretch. Assistant golf pros start at $35,000, and head golf pros make around $100,000. And while all your friends are jetting off to spend their weekends in the Hamptons or Malibu, you're stuck at home waiting for him to get off work. One thing to keep in mind: There's actually nowhere else he'd rather be! Golf pros live for golf season, and they absolutely love anything and everything golf related. When he's not teaching it, he's watching it, playing it, or talking about it. And when the two of you do get vacation time, don't expect him to leave his clubs behind.

Chances are he can't go one week without teeing off. Note: Most golf pros are incredibly honest and faithful.

Perks

Free golf clubs, clothes, bags, greens fees, you name it! Most golf pros get sponsored by a specific brand (i.e., Callaway), which means that the free stuff just keeps on coming. So just when you thought you could get him to put on a pair of Seven jeans and loafers, he gets a package in the mail with, guess what, more golf clothes! And what guy doesn't love the word *free* coupled with the word *golf*? Note: If he's PGA certified he will have access to some of the biggest golf tournaments, including the Masters. Yes, you can go too.

Will You Rule Him Out?

Before you decide, here's a look at what to expect when you are dating a PGA golf pro.

Rule #1:

He'll be hard to reach during the day.

Golf pros are pretty hard to pin down during the day, so don't take it personally if you call the pro shop and they tell you that he's on the course. Chances are they're telling the truth and not giving you the brushoff at his request. This guy is always running around during the day, which is part of the reason why he loves his job. He might have back-to-back lessons on the course, which means that he'll be out of touch for hours (they never bring their cell phones). So, if you leave a message, don't expect to hear back from him right away. Oh, and as for e-mail, he's rarely on that either. When he's not on the course giving a lesson he might be on the first tee making sure people are teeing off on time, in the bag room doing club repair, or at the clubhouse getting lunch. Hey, a guy's got to eat, right?

Rule #2:

He won't be able to take you away on the weekends.

Golf pros work every Saturday and Sunday of golf season, which is March through November for those on the East Coast and pretty much every day of the year for those who live in warm-weather climates. Not only does this mean that he won't be able to take you away on romantic summer weekends, but chances are you won't be staying up late on a Friday or Saturday night either. That's right, your all-American golf pro has to be at work by 7 A.M. sharp. "This is really hard and I get depressed before summertime every year because I know that while all the other couples are getting ready to enjoy the good weather and travel to little romantic places on the weekend, we are stuck at home. During golf season he works six days a week, including Saturdays and Sundays. And his one day off is Monday, which is when I am working. So, we really don't get to see each other much," says Lori. "Yes, we can have a nice dinner Friday night but he has to get up at 6:30 A.M. the next morning. It definitely can get a little lonely. " The good news is that during the off-season (when it's too cold for golf), golf pros tend to work four to five days a week (though they still work Saturdays), but their hours are substantially less. Plus, it's much easier to get in touch with them given that they spend most days in the pro shop.

Rule #3:
Women will flirt with him during their private lessons.

We've heard it all before—the married woman who has an affair with her golf pro. Though this is known to happen (especially in private sessions; see Chapter 20, "The Personal Trainer"), it's not a particularly common occurrence (note: many more trainers have affairs with their clients than golf pros), so don't get all panicked and jealous! Most golf pros are incredibly professional, clean-cut, "play by the rules" kinda guys who would much rather play golf than play around with someone else's wife.

Rule #4:

His most stressful time is when he's studying for the PGA certification exam.

This is probably the only time you'll see him stressed and under pressure, so if you're just starting out in your relationship, be patient with him. The PGA professional certification exam involves three parts and it's incredibly competitive and psychologically demanding. There's a written exam, which he has to take in Florida; an oral presentation, which he gives in front of a number of judges; and a thirty-six-hole playing test, which he can do at his own golf club (some people take this twenty times before they pass). Chances are he'll spend hours on the golf course practicing for his playing test, and then many more hours taking the test and failing. "I used to wait by the phone all day, knowing that he was out on the golf course taking that playing test," says Lori. "It's so psychologically demanding to spend all those hours playing only to realize that your score just isn't good enough. It would be heart-wrenching sitting at work having no idea whether or not he was playing well that day. And then he'd call as soon as he got off the course to tell me that he'd failed, again. Some people have to take these playing tests twenty times before they pass, and it becomes so psychological. That was the most stressed I'd ever seen him. And when he finally did pass, he called me at the office and I was in a meeting with my boss. When he told me the news and I just burst into tears, my boss thought someone had died! But the truth was, I knew how badly my boyfriend wanted this and I was just so happy for him."

Rule #5:
He will be a genuinely positive, calm, and patient individual.

Golf is one of the most difficult and frustrating sports to learn, as you may well know. It's anything but immediate and far from rewarding, at least those first few years. Now imagine your guy out there every day, working with beginners, whether they be powerful businessmen who hate failing at anything but know they must learn the game in order to network outside the office, or the wives of golf fanatics who realize that unless they learn the game, they are going to end up divorced. Whatever the case may be, your guy has to be extremely positive, informative, encouraging, and patient with these people. And all those qualities translate into his personal life as well (chances are he'll make a great dad). Just make sure he doesn't get too used to the role of instructor. He may know golf, but that doesn't mean he's the expert on everything.

Rule #6:
These guys are typically very neat and anal.

Think about it. They spend their lives studying the speed of the greens, the slope of the course, the direction the wind blows, their stance, grip, follow-through, and everything else they can think of when playing this game. Can you imagine if football players had to choose from nine different footballs before each play? It would be ridiculous! There is no other sport out there that's so exacting and detailed, and so very slow at the same time. So what does this mean for you? Chances are your guy is extremely neat, organized, and careful. "They are all so focused when they get out there. Everything has to be perfect and they have no problem taking their precious little time before every shot to make sure that everything is lined up and in its perfect place," says Alison. "I am much too impatient and impulsive for the game."

Rule #7:
He will talk about golf all the time.

When he's not teaching it, he'll be playing it, and when he's not playing it, he will be watching it—and when he's not watching it, he'll be talking about it. Oh, and when he does take time off to take you on a vacation, expect him to bring his clubs with him, because chances are, he can't make it a week without playing the game! Expect your guy friends to love this guy. Your friend's boyfriends will drill him with questions, asking which golfers he's met, who he's played with, where he played, how to perfect their swing, you name it. "Everyone who comes over to the house always ends up talking golf with him," say Kate. "And they get so excited about it too. It can get frustrating but I know how much he loves it, and I guess that becomes part of his charm. Still, you have to be prepared to hear about golf all the time."

Teed Off?

Tired of waiting for him to get off the greens? Here are a few golf resorts he's sure to love, and guess what? You won't mind them so much either.

- **Lodge at Koele, Lanai, Hawaii:**

  What he needs to know: The seventeenth hole has a 200-foot drop from tee to green (very cool!).

  What you need to know: The weather is amazing, the beaches are beautiful, and the accommodations are luxurious.

- **Four Seasons Resort Hualalai, Big Island:**

  What he needs to know: The fairways are contoured by the lava fields.

  What you need to know: You're staying at a Four Seasons; what more do you need to know!

- **Rimrock Resort Hotel, Banff, Alberta:**

  What he needs to know: There are five amazing golf courses to choose from, all with breathtaking views of the Canadian Rockies.

  What you need to know: The resort has beautiful rooms, a full-service spa, indoor pool, tennis, horseback riding, and hiking trails.

- **Westin Resort and Spa, Whistler, British Columbia:**

  What he needs to know: There are spectacular views, including an elevation change of over 400 feet. The Chateau Whistler Golf Club is carved from the side of Blackcomb Mountain.

  What you need to know: The resort offers a full-service spa, fine dining, spectacular hiking, biking, white-water rafting, and of course, shopping.

He Says . . .

Make summer weekend plans.

"This is the biggest challenge I've had with my past girlfriends. Everything will be great until the summer comes and then they get pissed off that I can't take off work and be with them. I understand that it's annoying, but there are so many guys out there that have to travel a lot for business or stay at the office until 3 in the morning only to come home stressed and deflated. Things could be much worse. I know because these are the guys that come to the golf course to play every Saturday and Sunday. My best advice is to make some plans ahead of time. At much as we'll miss you, it's okay to go to the beach with friends for the weekend. I know it's not ideal, but it's better than being bored and miserable, and making us miserable."—Brett

This is the job that was meant for me—I could never survive at a desk job.

"Most of the guys I work with feel the same way. We wouldn't want to do anything else with our lives. Sure, we won't make the salary of a banker, but we also would never trade our lifestyle for theirs. We all see them here on the weekends and they are so stressed out and jealous of what we do. A golf pro needs a woman who loves what he does and realizes that it's perfect for him. It also helps if she loves the game!"—Charles

She Says . . .

Expect him to carry at least one club wherever he goes.

"It's like his blankie. Whatever the reasoning, get used to it. No matter what we are discussing, even if it's pretty serious, he will be perfecting his stance and practicing his swing. And when I get annoyed, he'll tell me that it soothes him and helps him think. He's actually hit me twice by accident! Finally I realized that he needs his own space for everything golf. Now I've got him set up in the basement with all his golf paraphernalia, including this huge PGA rug, an artificial putting green, and at least ten staff bags. Still, I can't get him to keep his clubs down there!"—Lori

Learn to play golf or at least learn about the game.

"I don't really like it so much but I'm jealous of my friends who do because they go out there and play with their husbands and boyfriends. At least I am independent. If you're not independent and you don't like your space, my advice is to get out there and learn that game. This way you'll be able to enjoy it together. The truth is that even though I don't play much, I do know about the game, the players, and the tournaments, and so I can watch them with him. Also, golf pros are the best guys. They are just quality guys who are doing what they love."—Corey

Talking Shop

Here's a list of key words and phrases that will help you speak his language:

Back nine: The last nine holes of an eighteen-hole course. If he calls you from the course and tells you he's on the back nine, it means he's more than halfway done with the game!

Birdie: No, this has nothing to do with birds. A birdie is a golf term used to describe his score on a particular hole. If he birdies a hole he gets the ball in the hole in one stroke under par. Just know that this is a good thing.

Bogey: The opposite of a birdie. If he bogeys a hole he is one stroke over par for the hole, which is not a good thing.

British Open: The National Championship put on by the Royal and Ancient Golf Club of St. Andrews, Scotland. If your guy is PGA certified, chances are he'll be able to get into this tournament, which might mean a mini-vacation for you! Regardless of whether the two of you go, he will be obsessed with watching it. Translation? You won't see him much during this four-day period.

Bulge: Oh stop! He's not talking about your stomach. Instead he's talking once again about his clubs. The bulge of a club refers to the curve across the face of a wooden club.

Bye: A term used in tournaments. The player who draws a bye is allowed to advance to the next round without playing an opponent. If your boyfriend draws a bye, he should be able to leave the golf course and spend the day with you.

Choke: No, he's not a mass murderer nor is he someone who screws up under pressure. Choke refers to his grip on the club. If your guy tends to choke the club it just means that he grips down farther on the club handle.

Drive: Don't be fooled, this has nothing to do with you driving the golf cart, so get back out there and start swinging. To drive the ball means to hit the ball with maximum force and full stroke. Usually a drive is hit with a (duh!) driver (which is the name of the club), and usually it's hit from the tee.

Driving range: Where your boyfriend goes when he's not playing golf or watching it on TV. The driving range is an area or building used for the purpose of practicing tee shots and other strokes.

Front nine: The first nine holes of an eighteen-hole course. In other words, if he's still on the front nine, he's not even halfway done with the game.

Greens fee: Though you might not believe it, playing golf can be a pretty costly hobby. Greens fees are the fees that clubs charge for you to play the course, and sometimes it's upward of $400. The good news is that if you're dating a PGA golf pro, chances are he won't have to pay (or at least he'll get a major discount).

Green jacket: Who would have thought that men would be lusting after a hunter green blazer? The green jacket is the prize given to the winner of the Masters Tournament. Your boyfriend will daydream about winning the famous green jacket.

chapter 20

The Personal Trainer

There are two types of personal trainers, and within seconds of meeting them you should be able to tell the difference. The first is the borderline meathead. He's tan, buff, vain, macho, and a little rough around the edges. There's a definite cheesy side to this business and the meathead trainer falls right into that category. This guy can be found strutting around the gym like he owns the place, complete with a clipboard in his hands and a stopwatch around his neck. When he's not working one-on-one training a client, he can be found drinking protein shakes, shooting the shit with the other trainers, checking out his body (and his new tattoo) in the mirror, working out, schmoozing with the gym rats (AKA, gym members who spend way too much time at the gym), or lying on the roof deck catching some rays, assuming it's warm outside. This guy practically lives at the gym, and why wouldn't he? It's the one place where women in spandex and tight tank tops flock to him to ask him every question from "Could you spot me?" to "How much do you charge an hour?"

The second type of trainer is more conservative and professional. Chances are he has a number of certifications, including a college degree in something like exercise and nutritional science. And many of these guys are actually athletes, whether they played college football, ran track, or competed on the swim team or wrestling team. These guys can also be found at the gym, with the clipboard and the stopwatch. The difference is that they take their job more seriously and many of them are certified in things like rehab and prenatal care.

Thinking of dating either one of these guys? Before you do, find out how many other women he's currently dating, and what his goals are. Oh, and make sure you're not the jealous type, because regardless of who he is or how many tattoos he has, this guy will spend his days working on other women's bodies while listening to their most intimate secrets.

His Look

He cares about it. This guy has more pairs of sneakers than you have cute night-on-the-town shoes. Chances are he'll spend his days in workout gear and his nights in a fashionable pair of jeans and a fitted shirt (yes, he wants people to see his muscles). His apartment, no matter how big or small, will include a few more mirrors than the average guy, and of course, a set of dumbbells.

Though he cares a lot about his looks, he's not necessarily a neat freak, so don't be surprised if he doesn't make his bed in the morning. When he's not at the gym fighting off all the women in spandex, he can be found glancing at himself in the mirror, checking out his body from every angle. Most likely he's more obsessed with his body than he is with yours, although he cares if you're in good shape. Plus he's incredibly active, and he'll want you to be active too. Note: Trainers might not make a lot of money, but for some reason they always carry around a lot of cash.

His Vibe

Confident and in charge. The meathead ones tend to be a bit more macho and cocky, always trying to prove their masculinity by either shouting at their clients in a boot camp sort of "get down and give me ten more" kind of way (which could be sexy), or by doing ten pull-ups in the middle of their training session (which could be annoying). Regardless, trainers love to hear themselves talk and are very proud of their work—they all think they've created the best class, the best new exercise program, the best eating regime. Many of them will consider themselves entrepreneurs. Expect him to tell you all about his bigger, loftier goals like opening up his own gym, starting his own clothing line, or becoming the next Billy Blanks. Whether he follows through with his entrepreneurial ventures is a different story.

His Hours

Early mornings (he'll be up and out of the apartment by 6 A.M. every morning) with a three-hour break to nap or run errands once 9 A.M. hits and the corporate world takes off for work. As for the rest of the day, expect his lunch hours (12 to 2 P.M.) to be booked with clients followed by free afternoons, unless he teaches classes, takes classes, or has a second job like acting, modeling, coaching teams, etc. Unfortunately most of his evenings are spent training clients after work, so chances are he won't be free to see you until after 9 P.M. If you work a typical nine-to-five job, you won't be able to see your guy that often—unless you stalk him at the gym, which could make you extremely jealous; remember, his job is to make his clients feel special, not you.

Risk Factor

You don't really know where he is all day or who he's training (he could be spending hours alone with anyone from a supermodel to an overweight mother who just gave birth). Add to that the fact that trainers make up their own schedules, which makes it easy for him to lie about his whereabouts. Worse, when he's not training at the gym he could be training someone in the privacy of her very own home! This is actually pretty normal. Expect your guy to get hit on by lonely women who'll hire him for his attention and encouragement, or hot women who think he's sexy and want to get with him. Oh, and don't be surprised if his clients tell him intimate secrets about their dating life. It's a known fact that clients tell their trainers everything, from their secret sexual fantasies to the last person they had sex with.

Perks

He's strong and fit, which means you'll feel safe and protected. Plus, if the two of you are really serious, chances are you'll get a free gym membership, or at the very least, a free monthly pass complete with your own private coach/trainer (yes, he will train you, even at times when you don't want to be trained). Expect to be in the best shape of your life when the two of you are together. This guy loves to be physically active and he will expect you to be active as well. These guys also tend to be very sexual. They study the body and they know where all the pressure points are. Note: Some of these guys are certified massage therapists.

Is he a meathead or a professional trainer?

Though some of these guys are certified trainers with fitness degrees, others chose this career to pass the time, meet women, work on their bodies, and make extra cash. Here's how to tell them apart:

- Is he certified by the ACSM (American College of Sports Medicine), or the NSCA (National Strength and Conditioning Association)?
- Does he check himself out in the mirror more than three times during one training session?
- Does he reveal way too much information about his sex life during your sessions?
- Does he check out and flirt with other women while he's training you?
- Does he spend his spare time working as a model, an "exotic dancer," or a struggling actor?
- Is he ripped to the point of being unattractive?

Will You Rule Him Out?

Before you decide, here's a look at what to expect when you are dating a personal trainer.

Rule #1:
If you're casually dating a trainer at your gym, chances are he's casually dating a lot of other women at the gym too.

If he's good-looking, this guy will probably get hit on a lot. Whether he's teaching popular classes that a lot of women attend or he simply hangs out at the gym a lot, leaving his schedule open for new clients, expect your guy to get tons of attention. Think about it. This is the place where everyone comes to prance around in their spandex, improve their bodies, boost their self-esteem, and meet people. And these women have the perfect excuse to talk to a hot trainer; they want to inquire about personal sessions. "One time I was casually seeing six different women from the gym and all six showed up for the same class I was teaching! That was a little insane," says Joe. "There were about thirty people in the class and these women were all spread out in the front row staring at me and trying to make eye contact. And the whole time I was thinking to myself, how do I get out of this class when it's over?"

Rule #2:
Make sure you trust this guy, because he will develop intimate relationships with his female clients.

It's not uncommon for trainers to train clients in their private homes, so make sure you trust this guy. He has every opportunity in the world to cheat on you. Plus, there's no way to know where he is every day, and lots of times he won't answer his cell phone. "I remember how hard it was going to the gym every day, watching him train these hot little women who so obviously loved his attention," says Rachel. "You have to be extremely secure if you're going to date a trainer, regardless of whether he's a trainer at your gym or somewhere else. First, because he has an awesome body and women love that, and second because he's surrounded by women in spandex every day. My ex-boyfriend used to tell me about his female clients and everything they revealed to him and it was pretty insane. There are no boundaries between clients and trainers. Seriously, these guys don't have any problem discussing their clients' sex lives with them, and the clients have no problems sharing that information. I think there's this odd sexual tension between trainers and their clients because so much time is focused on your body. It's also very hands-on. Though I am not saying there's any reason to worry if you have a good guy, I am saying that you can't be too jealous of a person because the last thing he'll want is for you to be suspicious and questioning him all the time."

Rule #3:
Be prepared to change gyms.

Before you get involved with a trainer at your gym, ask yourself this: Are you willing to change gyms if things don't work out? Because if things don't end up working out, chances are you're going to be miserable seeing your ex every time you go to the gym, and watching him flirt with other women. So, before you get involved, check out your neighborhood and make sure there's an alternative if things don't work out. "There is nothing more annoying than going to your gym after the two of you break up," says Laurie. "First, because he looks so hot in whatever he's wearing and you have to see that every day. And second, because he will watch you when you talk to other guys. Plus, regardless of whether you even see him there, it's just not relaxing, which makes your workouts that much harder."

Rule #4:
He will have to work odd hours and most weekends.

Trainers are at the beck and call of their clients, which means they work around their clients' schedules. What does this mean for you? Most likely he'll be busy when everyone else is free. And yes, that includes the weekends. Trainers work early mornings (before their clients go to work), midafternoon (when their clients are free to duck out of work for lunch), and in the early evening (when their clients get out of work). So, don't expect to have breakfast, lunch, or dinner with this guy, unless you meet him in the neighborhood in between his training sessions. As for the rest of his day, he has huge chunks of free time, which are usually spent schmoozing with other trainers and members, working on his own body, or in his apartment napping. Of course, if he's motivated he'll probably use his free time to study for additional certifications, write a business plan for his new business venture (every trainer has plans to open his own business), or training for a triathlon.

Rule #5:
He will want you to be physically active.

This guy loves exercise and chances are he's learned everything from kickboxing to mountain climbing. Trainers love to learn new ways to stay in shape, and they enjoy challenging themselves. And he will want to do these kinds of things with you too. "We used to run around the reservoir twice a week, and he would be coaching me the whole way," says Jodi. "It was actually great. I was in the best shape of my life. Plus, there's something very appealing about being coached. It's this amazing feeling of being taken care of; whether that's the case or not is a whole other story. Still, it felt like he was always helping me, paying attention to me, and challenging me to push myself."

Rule #6:
Yes, he will want you to be at his triathlons.

Most likely this guy will compete in biathlons, triathlons, mini-marathons, you name it. Though he won't expect you to compete with him (although he'd *love* it if you did), he will expect you to be out there with him (rain or shine), cheering him on and taking pictures of him every time he runs by or bikes past you. Yes, it is a major turn on to see him out there in his gear with a number on his chest, but it's also a major drag to get up at 5 A.M. on a Saturday morning to help him cart around his equipment (i.e., wetsuit, goggles, bike shoes, helmet, nutrition bars). Prepare to spend hours waiting around, with a camera in your hand, for that one moment that you can scream out his name while trying to take his picture.

Rule #7:

He will critique your workout, even when you don't want him to.

This is not his fault. He's so used to telling people what exercises to do and how to do them that it will be difficult for him to stand by and watch you do something the wrong way. "I'd get home from a long day at work and all I'd want to do is get on the StairMaster and zone out. Instead, Jeff would be right next to me and every time I'd lean on those handrails, he'd tap my arm and tell me to stop. Ugh! I wanted to kill him," says Laurie. "Plus, when we'd go to do sit-ups or pushups, he'd be like, 'Come on, you know you can do more than that. Just give me one more set.' It was great most of the time, but sometimes you just want to be left alone, even if it means having a light workout."

He Says . . .

At the gym women come on to men.

"A lot of the women I date come up to me first. One woman wanted me to train her and it took her two months of us training together before she asked me out. I thought for sure she had a boyfriend, and I am not one of those prying trainers. But then we started to really hit it off and it's true, you do become close with someone when you are working together two or three times a week for an hour each time.

Anyway, eventually she asked me out. She told me that she had a crush on me and that's why she asked me to train her. I had to stop training her once we started dating though, because it's hard to charge your girlfriend."—Joe

Not all trainers are cheesy.

"There's definitely a rough-around-the-edges, cheesy side to this industry, but it depends on which gym you go to. The more luxurious gyms and clubs hire more professional people with numerous certifications and specialties. It's the cheaper gyms that have those young guys that are just doing this to pass the time, beef up, and meet women. Don't make assumptions until you get to know us."—Jeff

She Says . . .

Some guys get stuck being personal trainers.

"It seems like a lot of my boyfriend's friends started out as personal trainers when they graduated from school or maybe they did it part-time for extra cash when they were in school, and then they just got comfortable. It can be a pretty nice lifestyle for a while. I remember his first year out of college when all of his friends were stuck behind their desks, pulling all-nighters, and he'd be out in the park running with clients, meeting new people, staying active. He loved it and he couldn't understand why his friends were doing what they were. Now they're making hundreds of thousands of dollars and flying around the world meeting all sorts of important people, and I think that's hard for him."—Maria

Trainers are very sexual people.

"He was by far the most intense sexual relationship I've ever had. I think more than any other guy, especially the lawyers, doctors, and bankers, the personal trainer prides himself on being able to please his girlfriend. Expect everything from candles and massage oils to two-hour lovemaking sessions. And I think that's a pretty safe statement because I have two other friends who also dated trainers, and they've had similar experiences. They're very in touch with their bodies and it makes them feel manly when they can please a woman in bed, whereas the other guys feel manly when they make good money or do something amazing at work."—Charlotte

The Breakdown

Here's the skinny on the personal trainer:

biggest turn on	His body
biggest challenge	Your body (he has high expectations)
best way to get in touch	Cell phone
greatest perk	Flexible hours (perfect for a midday quickie), and he's very sexual
best timing	Anytime

Talking Shop

Here's a list of key words and phrases that will help you speak his language:

Certified strength and conditioning specialist (CSCS): A specific certification that serious trainers achieve. In order to acquire this your boyfriend must pass a rigorous two-part exam: one part consists of 80 multiple-choice questions in the areas of exercise sciences (anatomy, exercise physiology, biomechanics, etc.) and nutrition; and the other part is a practical section, which consists of 110 multiple-choice questions pertaining to program design, exercise techniques, testing, and evaluation. All you need to know is that he'll be really busy during this time.

Cellulite: As if any of us need to know the formal definition! Still, it's fat stored beneath the skin. Sadly, it has a dimpled appearance caused by the structure of the skin fiber that covers it. Gross.

Contraction: He's not referring to a client's labor pains. When he talks about a contraction, he's speaking about the tightening of a specific muscle.

Cool-down period: AKA, your favorite part of your workout. The cool-down period is the end of a workout when the body slowly cools down to a nearly normal temperature. Though you might look forward to this part of your workout, you might dread this part of his client's workout. Some trainers stretch their clients as part of the cool-down. Don't be surprised to find them both on a massage table with her legs in the air.

Crunches: Those abdominal exercises that you know you need to be doing more of. Crunches are a big favorite for trainers, so start doing them.

Daily log: Think *Bridget Jones's Diary* minus the sexual escapades. A daily log is a diary of daily activity or eating patterns. Some trainers want you to keep one of these. Just make sure he doesn't keep one for himself. There's something strange about a guy who documents what he eats all day.

Delayed onset muscle soreness (DOMS): We've all experienced this and it sucks. Just when you think you've had a good workout without any residual pain, it creeps up on you. DOMS is muscle soreness that occurs twenty-four to forty-eight hours after intense exercise.

Dumbbell: No, we are not referring to your trainer boyfriend. A dumbbell is a free weight used for exercising.

Dynamic flexibility: Chance are he's dynamically flexible, which is good news for you. It means he'll have a wide range of motion.

Empathy: The ability to understand another person's point of view in a manner that still allows objective reasoning. Most trainers are so good at being empathetic that their clients feel comfortable sharing the most intimate details of their lives. Hopefully he's able to empathize outside of the gym as well.

Endorphin: A natural chemical released by the body during exercise. Endorphins help relieve pain and leave his clients with a natural high. They also make you horny (another reason why a trainer's job is risky).

Flex: The contracting or tightening of a muscle. Chances are your trainer boyfriend will love to "flex" his muscles in your presence. Just make sure he's not doing it in front of the mirror.

Form: The manner in which a particular exercise is performed. Trainers are very big on form. Expect him to critique your form even when you are not in the mood to be "trained." This is kind of inevitable. Bad form is a trainer's biggest pet peeve.

Muscle head: A term used to describe a person who works out in the gym all the time and has become quite muscular; often used in a derogatory manner.

Triathlon: A race with three parts: a swim, a bicycle ride, and a run. Chances are your trainer boyfriend will participate in these. What does this mean to you? Expect to get up at 5 A.M. with a smile on your face and a camera in your hand, because you'll be the one taking his picture.

Conclusion

Okay, so now you have a better idea about what all these guys are doing all day. Finally you know why the talent agent never answers his office phone (that's his assistant's job), the consultant always calls you from the airport (he travels constantly), and the lawyer cancels plans at the last minute (he has no control over his schedule). Plus, you know your potential guy's good points (of which he has many) as well as things to expect that you shouldn't take personally, like your doctor boyfriend being on call on the night of your birthday. So, even though no one can fully prepare you for the guy you're about to fall for (hey, no one said all these guys were the same), hopefully we've given you enough material to proceed with caution. After all, there are good guys and bad guys in all fields and in the end it's up to you to decide what you can and can't live without. Sure, you might fall in love with a successful investment banker and be loaded, but if you're not independent and he's never around, will it really be worth it? Only you will know. Remember this: No matter how strenuous, time-consuming, or isolating your man's job is, if he is worth your time at all, he'll find the time, energy, and resources to treat you right!